DR. KAY KUZMA

Other books by Dr. Kay Kuzma

- *180 Power Tips for Parents*

- *Belonging: Overcoming Rejection and Discovering the Freedom of Acceptance*
  (Nancy and Ron Rockey with Kay Kuzma)

- *Between Hell and High Water—God Was There: Survival Stories From Hurricane Katrina*
  (Kay Kuzma and Brenda Walsh)

- *Easy Obedience: Teaching Children Self-discipline With Love*

- *The First 7 Years: Parenting With Strong Values and a Gentle Touch*

- *Mending Broken People: 3ABN Miracle Stories*

- *Parenting Boot Camp: Basic Training for Raising Responsible Kids*

- *Passionate Prayer Promises: More Than 100 Prayers and Scriptures That You Can Pray, Claim, and Believe* (Brenda Walsh and Kay Kuzma)

- *Prayer Promises for Kids: More Than 100 Prayer Promises to Pray, Claim, and Believe*
  (Kay Kuzma and Brenda Walsh)

- *Serious About Love: Straight Talk to Single Adults*

For information on Dr. Kay Kuzma's other resources, visit **www.FamilyResourceRoom.com**.

180 Power Tips for Marriage

DR. KAY KUZMA

3ABN | books

Pacific Press®
Publishing Association

Nampa, Idaho | Oshawa, Ontario, Canada
www.pacificpress.com

Original design concept by Chrystique Neibauer | cqgraphicdesign.com
Cover by Steve Lanto
Inside by Kristin Hansen-Mellish

The author assumes full responsibility for the accuracy of all facts and quotations cited in this book.

Additional copies of this book are available from two locations:
Adventist Book Centers®: Call toll-free 1-800-765-6955 or visit http://www.adventistbookcenter.com.
3ABN: Call 1-800-752-3226 or visit http://www.store.3abn.org.
3ABN BOOKS is dedicated to bringing you the best in published materials consistent with the mission of Three Angels Broadcasting Network. Our goal is to uplift Jesus Christ through books, audio, and video materials by our family of 3ABN presenters. Our in-depth Bible study guides, devotionals, biographies, and lifestyle materials promote whole person health and the mending of broken people. For more information, call 618-627-4651 or visit 3ABN's Web site: www.3ABN.org.

ISBN 13: 978-0-8163-4437-6
ISBN 10: 0-8163-4437-X

13 14 15 16 17 • 5 4 3 2 1

How to Get the Most Out of Your Power Tips

Marriage is a twenty-four-hour-a-day job. Every minute is crammed with things that must be done to maintain a family. But you can give only so much without refilling yourself with thoughts to help you refocus your priorities and reflect on what God may be trying to say to you and your mate through His Word.

That's why I've written this practical daily inspirational guide filled with power tips that can be read in a minute or less. Each practical suggestion is tied to a Bible verse that can change your life and revitalize your marriage, if you will reflect on it and allow God's Spirit to impress you with how you can apply it. God created marriage—and He can re-create yours.

> *And He answered and said to them, "Have you not read that He who made them at the beginning 'made them male and female,' and said, 'For this reason a man shall leave his father and mother and be joined to his wife, and the two shall become one flesh'? So then, they are no longer two but one flesh. Therefore what God has joined together, let not man separate"*
> *(Matthew 19:4–6, NKJV).*

May this be your experience as you daily apply the wisdom, understanding, and knowledge of God to your family. One minute a day can change your life—if it's a God-inspired minute!

What Is True Love?

"Love is a many-splendored thing," is how love is defined in the 1955 Academy Award–winning theme song of the movie by the same name. The words of the song continue, *Love is nature's way of giving, a reason to be living, the golden crown that makes a man a king.*

Others say, "Love is what makes the world go round." Or "Love and marriage go together like a horse and carriage." But we all know that is not necessarily so. Marriage may start out with enough romance for a couple to think they're in love, but when tough times hit, disappointments loom, and dreams fade, often the love the couple thought they had for each other fades too.

Here's the best definition of love I've ever read: "True love is not physical or romantic. True love is acceptance of all that is, has been, will be, and will not be."

In other words, regardless of the circumstances, regardless of how bad things get, regardless of how couples might feel at the moment, true love never fails.

May the love you share with each other be *true* love!

"Love is patient and kind. Love is not jealous or boastful or proud or rude. It does not demand its own way. It is not irritable, and it keeps no record of being wronged. It does not rejoice about injustice but rejoices whenever the truth wins out. Love never gives up, never loses faith, is always hopeful and endures through every circumstance."
—1 Corinthians 13:4–7, NLT

Complete People Make Whole Marriages

It sounds like a loving thing to say, "You make me complete." But watch out! Do the math! One plus one equals two. But does one-half plus one-half equal one? No! It adds up to much less!

As long as both husband and wife feel that together they are complete, it's likely they'll enjoy a long and happy marriage. But when one or both begins to need the other to make up for a deficiency, the marriage ceases to equal a whole. Two needy people who marry don't end up meeting each other's need to be complete, instead they drain each other!

So if you're moody, don't expect your spouse to meet all your emotional needs.

If you're a "messy," your spouse shouldn't have to pick up after you.

Are you habitually late? Don't blame your spouse for not getting you someplace on time.

Just because you're forgetful, your spouse shouldn't have to keep your calendar.

Couples with great marriages constantly work on self-improvement so in love they can offer more to each other, rather than feeling they have to fill in for a needy partner who refuses to help himself or herself.

"For in Him dwells all the fullness of the Godhead bodily; and you are complete in Him, who is the head of all principality and power." —Colossians 2:9, 10, NKJV

DR. KAY KUZMA

Praiseworthy Thinking

If you think something will go wrong, it probably will. If you see your life as half empty, instead of half full, it probably will be. If you feel that you're not worthy of the best, you probably will never get it! But you don't have to be a victim of your defective thinking.

You can turn the terrible into the terrific by claiming God's promises. You can be everything God designed you to be, if you only believe He is constantly working out His will in your life. You can be a positive thinker if you just dwell on the good things in life rather than the bad. Count your blessings instead of your failures and disappointments—and you'll find yourself enjoying a better marriage.

Satan has made sure that if you're not careful, you'll default to negative thinking. But you don't have to let the devil control you. Just follow the positive formula in Philippians 4:8 to think on things that are praiseworthy. Sure it's tough. But just like pure gold comes out of the fire that burns away impurities, good thinking comes out of the tough work of choosing to be positive regardless of the circumstances.

"Finally, brethren, whatever things are true, whatever things are noble, whatever things are just, whatever things are pure, whatever things are lovely, whatever things are of good report, if there is any virtue and if there is anything praiseworthy—meditate on these things." —Philippians 4:8, NKJV

Treat Marriage as a Career

What does it take to advance in your career? Dedication, sacrifice, skill. These are just three things, but when applied to the most important career of all—that of being a successful marriage partner—they can make all the difference in the world.

Meg and Jake were preparing for careers in nursing and law when they met in college and fell in love. A month after they graduated, they got married and started new jobs.

By the time they celebrated their first anniversary, they were each successfully climbing their own career ladders, but they were beginning to wonder what happened to their dream for a vibrant marriage. They were co-existing, but not really enjoying a growing relationship.

Over their anniversary dinner, Meg questioned, "I wonder how different our marriage would be if we put the dedication, sacrifice, and skill into it as we are putting into building our careers?"

"Why not give it a try? What could we lose?" Jake suggested.

By their second anniversary, their dedication, sacrifice, and relational skills they were applying to their marriage were paying off. Their dream for a vibrant life together was coming true. Good marriages don't happen by chance; they happen when marriage becomes a couple's most important career!

"Trust steadily in God, hope unswervingly, love extravagantly. And the best of the three is love."
—1 Corinthians 13:13, *The Message*

DR. KAY KUZMA

The Best of the Worst

One day a woman complained that her husband at times treated her like a child, making most of the decisions. "Well," her friend replied, "does he make bad decisions?"

"No," she answered.

"Does he squander the money?"

"No."

"Does he forbid you from going to church?"

"No."

"Does he carouse and come home drunk?"

"No."

"Does he beat you?"

Again, she replied, "No."

"Well, then you have the best of the worst! It seems to me that you have a lot more to be thankful for than to complain about!"

Do you ever complain about your husband or wife? Maybe you, too, have the best of the worst. Why not start reflecting on each other's positive traits, instead of the negative, and be thankful!

"In everything give thanks; for this is the will of God in Christ Jesus for you." —1 Thessalonians 5:18, NKJV

Forgive Each Other

One day I made a terrible mistake. I dented the fender of my husband's new dream car. I wanted to get it fixed before he got home, but when I called the body repair shops in town, none could work it in. I knew I was in trouble!

I dreaded having to tell Jan what I had done. So I told our kids to not tell their daddy. Instead, I wanted to tell him myself so I could explain how it happened and cushion his reaction.

But as soon as their daddy got home, they yelled, "Daddy, you won't believe what Mommy did today!"

"What did she do?" he asked.

"She dented the Mercedes!"

So by the time he gave me my usual hug and kiss, he already knew about my mistake. I told him I'd get it fixed immediately. "Don't worry about it," he said with a chuckle. "You might put another dent in it and then we can get both fixed at the same time."

We laughed, and he never again mentioned the incident. As far as I knew, I was forgiven and the dent, forgotten. That's love!

"If you forgive those who sin against you, your heavenly Father will forgive you. But if you refuse to forgive others, your Father will not forgive your sins." —Matthew 6:14, 15, NLT

DR. KAY KUZMA

Don't Be a "Drippy" Wife

S weetheart, don't wear brown shoes with a blue suit." *Drip!*

"The lawn needs mowing. How many times do I have to tell you?" *Drip!*

"Don't slurp your soup!" *Drip!*

"And I can't understand you when you talk with food in your mouth." *Drip!*

"If you'd just do it right the first time, you wouldn't have to do it again." *Drip!*

Wives don't like having to always tell their husbands what to do. They don't like having to constantly nag. But too often they feel it's their responsibility to help their husbands break bad habits, get things done, avoid embarrassing themselves, or make sure they will make a good impression on others. And so without thinking, they tell their husbands what to do.

The wisest man who ever lived said that it's better to live alone in an attic or the desert than with a complaining wife in a lovely home. (See Proverbs 21:9, 19.) And he should know—having seven hundred wives and three hundred concubines!

So, wives, if you don't want to be as annoying as a leaky faucet, think twice before correcting your husband. Ask, "Is what I'm about to say really necessary?" If not, bite your tongue and praise the Lord for the special man in your life—just the way he is!

"A nagging spouse is a leaky faucet." —Proverbs 19:13, *The Message*

8

Screaming Is Demeaning

Have you ever yelled at a dog, "Good dog!" and watched the dog cower as if it's about to be struck. When it comes to words, the tone of voice is just as important—if not more important. For example, the words "I love you" can have a completely different meaning if said in a questioning tone, with sarcasm, or by screaming.

In Ephesians 5, just before the apostle Paul instructs married couples on the importance of husbands loving their wives as Christ loves them and wives submitting to that love, Paul makes a comment about a healthy home atmosphere. He says couples should be filled with the Spirit and speak to each other in psalms, hymns, and spiritual songs.

The fruit of the Spirit is love, joy, peace, long-suffering, kindness, goodness, faithfulness, gentleness, and self-control. None of these traits are possible if you yell at each other. Instead, when you have something important to communicate, lower your voice. Smile and calmly say what's on your mind. When you do, it will be like music to the ears of your husband or wife and will lift his or her spirits. Screaming is always demeaning.

"It only takes a spark, remember, to set off a forest fire. A careless or wrongly placed word out of your mouth can do that. By our speech we can ruin the world, turn harmony to chaos, throw mud on a reputation, send the whole world up in smoke and go up in smoke with it, smoke right from the pit of hell." —James 3:5, 6, The Message

---

DR. KAY KUZMA

Dead-End Versus Option-Thinking

Do you sometimes feel that your mate is boring and your marriage is stuck in a rut? Wallowing in regret will get you no place. Instead, you can change a stale marriage into a stimulating one by changing your thinking from dead-end thinking to option-thinking.

Dead-end thinking is to immediately conclude, *It's impossible!* If you think something is impossible, you'll give up without even trying.

Instead, try option-thinking. *If it's possible, then how?* Next, list the creative ideas that come to mind. You'll be surprised at the result.

Jess and Kasy felt trapped because they never had enough money to do the things they really wanted to do. "We don't even have money for a vacation!" Kasy complained. *Dead-end thinking!*

Jess suggested listing the vacations they would like to take if money wasn't a problem. Just thinking of possibilities was exciting. "Now, let's pick one, and make it happen!"

After brainstorming, they made a plan and set a target date. Six months later they were sunbathing on the Gulf Coast.

Dead-end thinking is a great destroyer of marriages. Instead, turn your stale marriage into a stimulating one with option-thinking.

"Is anything too hard for the LORD." —Genesis 18:14, NKJV

A Promise a Day

Did you know a promise a day can keep divorce away? Get in the habit of asking each other, "What do you need from me today?" and then promise to do it! It's that simple.

Great marriages are built on two foundational pillars: *Trust* and *Thoughtfulness*. Making a promise and keeping it establishes trust. And doing something special each day for your mate is a great way to prove your thoughtfulness.

If she says, "Pray for me!" don't just say you will and go about your day as usual, and then on your way home suddenly remember your promise and put in a concentrated ten minutes. Instead, pray every hour and somehow let her know: text, call, e-mail.

If he says, "I'd like you and the kids to meet me at the park for supper. I'll pick up pizza and some drinks," don't promise and then an hour before park time, complain that it's too much work. Instead, be enthusiastic and plan your day in such a way that you can make it happen without overstressing!

Make promise-keeping a daily practice and enjoy a vital growing relationship.

"I can do all things through Christ who strengthens me." —Philippians 4:13, NKJV

DR. KAY KUZMA

Are You Brain-Dominate Compatible?

Do you enjoy learning facts, memorizing lists, systematically solving problems, organizing things, and thinking logically? If yes, you are probably left-brained. That means the left hemisphere of your brain is dominant.

If you learn better from pictures, concrete objects, direct involvement, and sometimes seem a little disorganized and forgetful, then chances are you're right-brained.

Did you know that you have probably married your opposite. During courtship, these differences might be appreciated, as the strengths of one help overcome the weaknesses of the other. But, if couples aren't careful, these differences can become frustrating.

Les is left-brained. He pays attention to small details and organization. Jasmine is, what Les calls, scatterbrained. She isn't really, she is just right-brained, and is much more interested in spontaneity and creativity than perfection. But what really bothers her is how picky Les is.

They are headed toward World War III, unless they accept each other's differences and try to incorporate the positive tendencies of their mate into their own behavior, even if it doesn't come naturally. Here's my counsel: Lighten up, Les. And Jasmine, work on being more organized.

"I applied my heart to know, to search and seek out wisdom and the reason of things." —Ecclesiastes 7:25, NKJV

God Created Intimacy

When God created the world, He spoke and everything came into existence, that is, until He created man. Instead of speaking, God bent over and touched the dirt to form Adam and then He gave him artificial respiration. In other words, He "breathed into his nostrils the breath of life" (Genesis 2:7). You might say the Father God kissed His son, Adam, to life.

With this type of intimate encounter, is it any wonder that God loved Adam—and Adam loved God? There is a significant difference in the quality of a relationship you have with someone you only speak to and with someone you touch and kiss!

Then to make a partner for Adam, God made Eve out of Adam—another act of intimacy, linking not only Adam and Eve in a one-flesh relationship with each other, but also with an everlasting oneness with Himself.

Obviously, man and woman were made for intimacy with each other—and God. It's like the three points of a triangle: the closer a husband and a wife get to their Creator, the closer they become to each other.

"Then the LORD God formed the man from the dust of the ground. He breathed the breath of life into the man's nostrils, and the man became a living person." —Genesis 2:7, NLT

DR. KAY KUZMA

Sex Was God's Idea

God created sex to be the expression of the type of love that would form a stable foundation for a family. In the beginning God's plan was not just for marriage, but for family as well. God put sperm within Adam and ova (eggs) within Eve, so that as they were expressing their most intimate one-flesh love to each other, their union could create children in their own image.

Notice, just as God stroked and kissed man into existence, He planned that this same intimacy would be a vital part of the creation of children. And then He instructed the first two lovers on earth to have sex—or as the Bible puts it, to "be fruitful and increase in number" (Genesis 1:28, NIV).

It is interesting to note that while God said about the rest of His creation, "it was good," after Adam and Eve were created God said, "It was *very good*" (verse 31, NIV).

So what does love have to do with family? Everything. Love was the reason God designed a human family. And a family is the result of love—or at least that was God's original plan.

The closer you follow that plan in your own marriage, the more fulfilled you will be.

"Then God blessed them, and God said to them, 'Be fruitful and multiply'." —Genesis 1:28, NKJV

Men Need to Feel Wanted

Women sometimes complain that their husbands are nonsupportive when it comes to the housework and taking care of the children. If you're feeling the same, don't do what comes naturally—like criticize and complain. And don't greet him at the door with a "honey-do" list: "Honey-do this." "Honey-do that." Pushing a man to become more involved in your world is counterproductive.

Instead, get your priorities straight. Who should be number one in your life? Hint: it's not the housework or the kids. Just how much attention and admiration have you given him recently? Have you complimented him, thanked him, and pleasured him? Do you spend time each day looking at him and really listening? Are you a willing and creative sexual partner?

A man must feel *wanted*—not just needed. And the more he feels wanted, admired, and desired by you, the more he will feel like meeting your needs. Change your priorities, and chances are your man will change his!

"My beloved put his hand by the latch of the door, and my heart yearned for him." —Song of Solomon 5:4, NKJV

DR. KAY KUZMA

A Role-Model Marriage

Regardless of the quality of your marriage relationship, it is going to have a tremendous influence on your children's lives. They are going to follow your example about how to act when they get frustrated or angry and about how to rejoice when something goes well. They're going to learn to talk like you and react like you. In all your daily interactions, you'll be teaching your children lessons that will affect the way they live their entire lives and specifically how to respond when they are married. They'll learn how husbands should treat their wives, and how wives should treat their husbands.

Children are not blank slates upon which we can write whatever we want. They're born with their own personalities and temperaments. But they are like sponges. Children absorb everything about their parents.

You can't choose whether or not to influence your child. *You will influence*. But you can choose whether your influence will be positive or negative.

Consider your marriage. Are you the kind of husband or wife that you want your child to grow up to be? If not, you better make some changes quickly!

"Avoid every kind of evil." —1 Thessalonians 5:22, NIV

Ten Ways to Cherish a Wife

Men, have you ever wished for a submissive wife? Well, I can tell you ten ways to cherish her, and the result may be just what you've been wishing for.

1. Sacrifice for her. Be willing to give up something that you would like to do in order to pleasure her.
2. Look at her, and really listen.
3. Say kind things about her to others.
4. Share her responsibilities. Surprise her with your thoughtfulness.
5. Let her know you admire her. Tell her how attractive she is.
6. Be polite—treat her like a lady.
7. Be an understanding father.
8. Open doors of possibility for her. Don't just think of your own advancement, think about hers.
9. Touch and take time to be alone with her.
10. Be the spiritual leader of the family.

If you'll do these things, you'll be surprised what a difference it can make.

"Husbands, love your wives and do not be bitter toward them." —Colossians 3:19, NKJV

DR. KAY KUZMA

Ten Ways to Cherish a Husband

Cherished men make wonderful husbands! I don't know how scientific this is, but I challenge you to try these ten things and see if it doesn't make a difference in your marriage.

1. Respect your husband. Let him know you look up to him.
2. Cut the nagging.
3. Don't interrupt him when he's in the middle of a project—like watching Monday Night Football.
4. Ask him before he leaves each morning, "Honey, what do you need from me today?" And carry your fair share of family responsibilities.
5. Let him know he is sexually attractive to you.
6. Be playful.
7. Keep yourself looking great.
8. Be willing to compromise.
9. Wake up cheerful, and give him a compliment before breakfast.
10. End the day with a back rub.

Cherished husbands make good lovers and great companions, I know I've got one.

"Wives, submit to your own husbands, as is fitting in the Lord." —Colossians 3:18, NKJV

Choosing the Positive

A number of years ago I got a traffic ticket on the road in front of our house. I felt terrible about it. When I called my husband at work, he said, "Well, that's not so bad!"

"Not so bad? This ticket is going to cost a lot of money and our insurance is going to go up."

"Well," he said, "I still don't think it's so bad."

"What do you mean?"

"Well, honey, it has been a long time since we've gotten a ticket and we've probably grown a little careless in our driving. Perhaps by you getting this ticket we'll be more careful and avoid an accident."

I had never thought about it that way. After I hung up, I turned to my secretary and said, "I've just gotten a traffic ticket, and I've saved my whole family from disaster!"

You see, there are always two ways to look at things. The negative—and the positive! Why not choose the positive?

"Rejoice in the Lord always. Again I will say, rejoice!" —Philippians 4:4, NKJV

DR. KAY KUZMA

Sparking up a Dull Marriage

Do you get depressed when you read books telling you that you've got to be a sexy wife and do crazy things like wrap yourself in cellophane to have a sizzling marriage?

Well, it's not the cellophane that turns on a man, it's the woman inside. And nothing works quite as well as a ten-second appreciation message. It may even bring, in record time, a love message back your way.

Start by mentioning the specific behavior (or item) you appreciate. Say how it makes you feel. And add a "Thank you."

That's simple enough. Try: "The car looks great. I feel special when you wash it for me. Thanks." Or, on a more personal level: "*Ummm,* I like it when you touch me in public. Thank you for making me feel so special."

However insignificant the behavior or item was in the beginning, its meaning will increase with praise. A short appreciation message is guaranteed to spice up your life.

Ten a day should keep divorce away!

"And give thanks for everything to God the Father in the name of our Lord Jesus Christ." —Ephesians 5:20, NLT

If I Were a Husband

If I were a husband, I'd take my wife in my arms each morning, hold her tight, and let her absorb my energy for the day. I'd encourage her, "Sweetheart, God has gifted you in incredible ways. You can do it!" And I'd open doors of possibility for her.

I'd notice her hairstyle, a new dress, or the things she accomplished during the day. I'd go to Taco Bell for the kids, if she didn't want to cook, or volunteer to make the salad or season the soup. And I'd keep myself looking good for her.

If I were a husband, I wouldn't keep my wife guessing. I'd break down and cry if I felt like it. And I'd let her know when I was discouraged, angry, or resentful. And I'd let her comfort me.

I'd take her advice, stop to ask directions, and thank her for correcting me and helping me to be a better person. But most of all I'd love her just the way she was!

"Husbands, love your wives, just as Christ also loved the church and gave Himself for her." —Ephesians 5:25, NKJV

DR. KAY KUZMA

If I Were a Wife

If I were a wife, I'd admire my husband as my prince in shining armor, the king of our domain, and the best lover in the world. I'd run to him when he comes in the door and smother him with kisses. I'd give him some private time to sort out the mail, check his messages, and put his briefcase away before giving him a cool drink and asking him if he would like to hear about my day.

If I were a wife, I would be his greatest cheerleader. I would be the president of his fan club. I would celebrate his successes and encourage him when he felt like he had failed. I would brag to my friends and family about what a wonderful guy I married. And I'd make sure he knew that he was number one in my life.

I'd pray for him, go fishing with him, and yes, I'd even sit down and watch football with him—if he wanted me to. I'd love him for who he was, for who he was becoming, and for what he'd never be. And every night, I'd kneel beside my bed and thank the Lord for giving me the man of my dreams and the love of my life.

"I am my beloved's, and my beloved is mine. He feeds his flock among the lilies." —Song of Solomon 6:3, NKJV

How Are You Spending Your Time?

Husbands and wives can choose either to spend their time on things or relationships. The temptation for most is to focus on things or others, rather than on their own relationship. When you've worked extra hours to buy a new car, people notice. Or if you spend your time dusting and picking things up, you can brag about a clean house. If you're not careful, however, housework and job responsibilities can consume all your time. And if there is any left, keeping up with friends on Facebook and Twitter can eat up the rest!

But if you spend that time walking in the park together, cuddled on the love seat reading to each other, or lying on a blanket on the lawn watching for falling stars, what do you have to show for it?

To make sure your mate feels like your first priority, limit the time you're willing to give to others and to things. Instead, focus on building your relationship by spending positive time together. Others might not notice the results, but the two of you will feel your love for each other grow, and the result will be a more vibrant and satisfying relationship.

"How do you know what your life will be like tomorrow? Your life is like the morning fog—
*it's here a little while, then it's gone." —*James 4:14, NLT

DR. KAY KUZMA

Borrowing the Love You Don't Have

My friend, Trish, had in-laws who spent the winter months at her home. The last day of their previous visit, Trish and her mother-in-law had a terrible argument, making it extremely difficult to communicate during the year. Trish dreaded having them come again.

The day the folks arrived for their long winter's stay, Trish was thinking, *If only I could borrow a little love than maybe I wouldn't have so much hate.* And then a thought came to her: *Why not borrow some love from God?*

The idea intrigued her. She purchased a present and smiled as she gave it to her mother-in-law. *It's a love gift from God,* Trish thought to herself, but her mother-in-law thought it was from Trish. And the flowers and card left in their room weren't from Trish—but the folks thought so.

The result was a sweet, cooperative mother-in-law. The two of them didn't always agree, but a little love—even though it was borrowed—sure made a difference.

Oh, by the way, this power tip works with more than mother-in-laws!

"You have heard that it was said, 'You shall love your neighbor and hate your enemy.' But I say to you, Love your enemies and pray for those who persecute you." —Matthew 5:43, 44, RSV

Make Homecoming Rewarding

Did you know some men can't even think of loving their wives when they get home because they can't stand the clutter, the dirty dishes in the sink, and the unmade beds? Others don't mind a little mess, as long as there's acceptance and respect. They want their mate to love them unconditionally and make them feel special. It's the bickering, complaining, criticism, and sarcasm that they can't stand.

Do you know what your mate needs to really make your house a home? Maybe you've been slaving away to have a spotless house and are too tired to greet him with a hug at the door. If you ask, you may find out that he doesn't mind a little clutter as long as he comes home to a happy wife. Or maybe, he thought being on time was essential, when all she wants is a romantic kiss and his willingness to help with the cooking or housework.

The atmosphere you create at your homecoming will likely set the tone for the rest of the evening. What would it take to increase your mate's level of joyful anticipation about getting home? Maybe it's time you asked!

"Let all things be done decently and in order." —1 Corinthians 14:40, NKJV

DR. KAY KUZMA

Love Versus Infatuation

It's easy to fall in love—you have this incredible longing to be together, you daydream about the person loving you and have nightmares of him or her loving someone else. But how can you be sure if this emotional high is really love? What is love anyway and how is it different from infatuation?

I once read that infatuation is thinking your lover is as handsome as Tom Cruise, the movie star; as intellectual as Albert Einstein, the genius, as amusing as Rodney Dangerfield, the comedian; as devout as Billy Graham, the evangelist; and as athletic as Hulk Hogan, the wrestler.

Love, however, is realizing your guy is as handsome as Albert Einstein, as intellectual as Hulk Hogan, as amusing as Billy Graham, as devout as Tom Cruise, and as athletic as Rodney Dangerfield—*but, sticking with him anyway!*

Love is something that doesn't come and go with your feelings. Love is something that you do. Love is a choice. Love is sticking with the person you've committed your life to, no matter what.

"[Love] bears all things, believes all things, hopes all things, endures all things. Love never fails."
—1 Corinthians 13:7, 8, NKJV

When Life Is Overwhelming, Retreat

I once had a mom ask, "How can I get control of my life? My three boys are constantly fighting, the baby is demanding, the house is a mess, and my husband is no help! I have to end up screaming to get someone's attention!"

My advice was to spend more time with her husband. Make him your first priority. Let him know that he is special.

"What? That's not fair!" she cried. "The children need me and he can take care of himself."

My reply was that after a hurricane, you don't worry about the shingles until you've shored up the foundation, and without a strong foundation a family can topple.

Then I suggested they make plans for a romantic weekend retreat for two and recommit their lives to each other and to working through their problems *together*.

Chances are they would both come home with renewed energy and some creative problem-solving ideas. Time away from the kids gives couples a new perspective on life. Every married couple needs to "retreat" occasionally.

"In all your ways acknowledge Him, and He shall direct your paths." —Proverbs 3:6, NKJV

DR. KAY KUZMA

Beware of the "Dip"

Within the first seven years, almost all marriages experience what is termed the "dip." It may come on slowly, like the setting of the sun, or it may be that one day it just hits—like lightning.

Regardless, the dip is characterized by the husband and wife looking at each other and asking, "Why did we get married? We're so different!"

The excitement is gone, communication is routine, differences are exaggerated, and life together is boring. They realize that some expectations when they got married will probably never be realized, and an irresistible urge comes over them to change each other.

When that happens, resist the "irresistible urge" and refer back to God's owner's manual for dealing with the differences. First, practice mutual submission by continuing to love and respect each other (Ephesians 5:21). Specifically, men, love your wives! And women, respect your husbands (verse 33)!

It's the only way out of the dip. And the view on the other side is fantastic!

"Nevertheless let each one of you in particular so love his own wife as himself, and let the wife see that she respects her husband." —Ephesians 5:33, NKJV

Love Creates Love

You promised to love each other forever. But sometimes it's easier to love through sickness and poverty than when you get tired, grouchy, and frustrated—and your spouse is acting like a spoiled brat!

Now here's the really tough part. The very best time to give love away is when you and your mate's love quotients are on empty and you're running on fumes. It doesn't make sense. Logic says you should think of yourself and reserve however little you have. Certainly the last thing you *feel* like doing is giving love away to someone who you feel doesn't deserve it! But the truth is that *love creates love*. And giving is the only way of getting yourself filled up again. Filling your partner with love will significantly increase the chances that you'll get something back.

Sure it's a risk. There is no guarantee that if you give a little love, you'll get something in return. But it's also true that *feelings follow actions*. Just the process of acting in a loving way will quite likely make you feel better. So the way I see it, you never lose if you give love away.

"This is My commandment, that you love one another as I have loved you." —John 15:12, NKJV

DR. KAY KUZMA

Celebrate Valentine's Day All Year

It's fun to celebrate love. But why reserve this celebration for one day a year?

Why not send her flowers to celebrate a "nonoccasion" such as taking the snow tires off the car, the great lasagna she made, or sending in the income tax?

On your next day off, take an hour to do some little jobs he wants done, such as cleaning the desk drawer, or mending his shirt.

Switch off the sport's channel, take her hand, and go for a leisurely walk together so you can enjoy God's beautiful world.

Tape a note on his mirror that says, "Hi, Handsome! You're looking at the man that Jeanie [or whatever your name is] loves with all her heart."

Or make a list of all the things you appreciate about her and leave it on her pillow.

If your work requires that you travel, make arrangements for her to go along.

There are so many ways to say, "I Love You." Why not celebrate all year?

"Admonish the young women to love their husbands." —Titus 2:4, NKJV
"Husbands, love your wives." —Ephesians 5:25, NKJV

Tough Times Can Make Tough Marriages

It's not necessarily the good times that draw couples closer; it's struggling to overcome the bad ones. It's meeting difficulties and together somehow making it; like when the tent blows down in the middle of the night, or the car breaks down a hundred miles from nowhere. These will be the times that you will recount at family reunions over the years.

Gary Smalley, a counselor and author, has said that when he was a young father he noticed that there was one common factor in strong, healthy families. They all went camping. So he determined his family was going to spend time camping. Then after years of challenging experiences, he realized it wasn't the camping that brought families together. It was the problems they overcame while camping. It's the memories they made. It's coming to the conclusion that, regardless of the circumstances, we can make it through together.

So face each problem with courage and a smile, knowing that it's just another pillar that's going to make your marriage strong.

"My brethren, count it all joy when you fall into various trials, knowing that the testing of your faith produces patience." —James 1:2, 3, NKJV

DR. KAY KUZMA

YOU Can Be Confrontive

Did you know that unless you are purposely praising your spouse, the word YOU takes on a confrontational tone. First, notice how YOU can emphasize the positive: YOU are really dependable. YOU are handsome. YOU make my heart beat a little faster. YOU always are so willing to share. YOU are a great dad. YOU make me proud to be your husband.

Did you feel the "punch" of a sentence starting with YOU? It makes your praise statement even more meaningful. That's great—as long as you keep your YOU statements positive, but the same thing happens with the negative.

If you want to deliver a backhanded jab to your partner, just confront him or her with a statement beginning with YOU. YOU need to be more careful. YOU should have thought about your actions first. YOU are just plain forgetful. YOU are always criticizing me.

If you want to avoid conflict, start your confrontive sentence with an I. For example, I get frustrated when I don't know when you are going to be home; I feel better when the bathroom is clean; I like it when we have time to talk; I enjoy eating without the TV on. And save your YOUs for praise.

"For by your words you will be justified, and by your words you will be condemned." —Matthew 12:37, NKJV

Bury the Bitterness

There is nothing that hurts more than when your mate falsely accuses you of something and won't listen to reason. Your immediate reaction is to fight back. This tactic, however, seldom leads to reconciliation.

What you want to avoid is becoming angry and bitter. These emotions are much more harmful to you than false accusations. You may think if you retaliate, you can control what your mate might say or do next. But that's not true. The only thing you can control is your own response.

So take a deep breath and determine to stop thinking vindictive thoughts. Instead, think of something kind and good. Next, follow the Golden Rule and do something nice for him or her, even though it's undeserved. Finally, pray that God will do His good work in your spouse's heart.

If, however, the accusations continue, there is a deeper issue that needs to be resolved—like jealousy or trust. Seek professional help to know how to bury the bitterness; but at the same time stand up for yourself and say, "You may not treat me like this!"

"What blessings await you when people hate you and exclude you and mock you and curse you as evil because you follow the Son of Man. When that happens, be happy! Yes, leap for joy! For a great reward awaits you in heaven. And remember, their ancestors treated the ancient prophets that same way." —Luke 6:22, 23, NLT

DR. KAY KUZMA

You Don't Have to Be Bossy

Is your bossy behavior getting in the way of having a meaningful marriage? Well, you might not think so, but I can guarantee that if you're bossy and controlling, your mate is hurting, and will either fight back or withdraw.

Here's the famous cop-out! "But I've been bossy since birth. That's just the way I am." Well, I have news for you. Negative traits that are inherited or have become learned habit patterns can be overcome. Here's what it takes:

1. Conviction: You've got to be convinced you want to change.
2. Plan: You have to have a plan, such as substituting kind, thoughtful words every time you're tempted to criticize.
3. Public resolution: Tell someone so he or she can support you and encourage you when you feel like giving up, or can remind you when you've failed.

If you fail, don't punish yourself with negative self-talk, like "Stupid, why can't you think before you act?" It takes courage and self-worth to change. Negative self-talk destroys both. Instead, apologize and tell yourself, "I can do all things through Christ who strengths me."

"Let all bitterness, wrath, anger, clamor, and evil speaking be put away from you." —Ephesians 4:31, NKJV

The Gift of Stillness

When was the last time you were completely still and not asleep? How long has it been since your body was at complete rest for maybe an hour or so, and your whole ambition was to restore your spirit by listening, thinking, or just taking in the sounds of nature that speak to your soul?

Today's lifestyle seems to demand every moment of our day. Work, family, social activities, and recreation all contribute to a daily schedule that doesn't allow time out for anything extra, especially if that "anything" is to all appearances "nothing" but stillness.

If you believe that you don't have time to regenerate your spirit, your marriage will suffer. You can only give to your partner that which you have yourself.

Lean back or lie down. Close your eyes. What are your innermost thoughts? Allow your mind to talk with your heart. Commune with your Creator. Picture in your mind the last hours of Jesus' earthly life and consider how much He loves you. Let God's peace flow over you.

We all *have* the time—if we'll just take it. Think of this gift of stillness as a present you give to yourself.

"Rest in the Lord, and wait patiently for Him." —Psalm 37:7, NKJV

DR. KAY KUZMA

Get to Know Jesus Better

Too many couples have the idea that if they just work harder on their marriage their problems will be solved. It's true that any successful relationship takes time and effort. But working on a good marriage should be the result of inner joy and desire rather than done with a "have to" attitude.

No husband wants his wife to respond because she has to. No wife wants her husband to bring her gifts because he has to. Actions, without loving motivation, are hollow and suspect. It's easy for a mate to question, "Why is he doing this?" or "What does she want this time?"

The secret is to understand where love comes from—and fall more deeply in love with the Source. God is love. Just check out John 3:16 and 1 John 3:1.

Why does having a closer relationship to God make you a better spouse? Because that which you behold you become.

If you're really serious about showing your mate genuine Godlike *agape* love, then why don't you take some time to get to know Jesus better by studying His Word together?

"But we all, with unveiled face, beholding as in a mirror the glory of the Lord, are being transformed into the same image from glory to glory, just as by the Spirit of the Lord." —2 Corinthians 3:18, NKJV

Fill Your Emotional Container With Joy

Think of yourself as an emotional container. There is only so much room inside you for feelings. When you are filled with negative feelings, it's difficult to experience anything positive.

One way to get rid of those troublesome negative feelings is to write them down. The process of dealing with the feeling takes it out of your emotional container, creating a void inside you.

Now you have two choices: either continue thinking about that negative feeling you wrote down so it has a chance to jump back inside you, or fill the void with something positive.

Start the filling process by thinking of something you are thankful about. Start with your spouse and begin listing all the blessings you have experienced in your marriage. As long as your mind dwells on something positive, it can't concentrate on the negative.

Continue this exercise until all the negatives have been changed to positives and your cup will overflow with joy.

"In Your presence is fullness of joy; at Your right hand are pleasures forevermore." —Psalm 16:11, NKJV

DR. KAY KUZMA

Lighten the Load on Your Heart

Medically speaking, your heart weighs approximately one pound or less and is about the size of your fist. How does something so small carry all of the burdens and stresses that come with normal family life, and still have strength to do its job?

The Creator of our hearts must have known they would sometimes be overburdened. Perhaps that's why He said that instead of trying to carry all our problems by ourselves we should take His yoke and let Him walk beside us, carrying on His shoulders the cares that could weigh us down.

One of the built-in benefits of marriage is that you don't have to go through life alone. You have someone with whom to share the load.

So, when you are tempted to hold on to worries and frustrations, think about your heart. Don't overburden it with stress. Instead, as a couple, kneel down together and give your worries to God, let Him walk beside you and lighten the load on your hearts.

"Take My yoke upon you. . . . For My yoke is easy and My burden is light." —Matthew 11:29, 30, NKJV

Get Out of Rat Races and Ruts

When life is a rat race, the routine boring, you don't have time for each other and you're beginning to feel sorry for yourself, play the "what if" game to discover some alternatives. For example, what would happen if you quit work or only worked part time or said, "No overtime?" What would happen if you went back to school or decided to change jobs or move? What would happen if you would took a second honeymoon or traveled across country on a motorcycle?

To play the game fairly you must remain open to a wide range of possible answers to each question you pose.

That's exactly what Bruce Bogan did. He was an aeronautics engineer; his wife an artist. They played the "what if" game, left big city jobs, and moved to the country. Bruce applied his engineering expertise to sculpturing. His success exceeded his wildest expectations. But the real benefit was more time with his wife and family and no more guilt.

If families like the Bogans can get out of life's rat races and ruts, you can too. Just remember it all starts with the question "What if . . . ?"

"If you have faith as a mustard seed, you will say to this mountain,
'Move . . .'; and nothing will be impossible." —Matthew 17:20, NKJV

DR. KAY KUZMA

Resolving Stubborn Resistance

Here's an experiment to try. Put your hands up and ask your mate to place his or her hands palm to palm against yours. Now push. How did the other respond? Chances are they pushed back!

That's a great object lesson for marriage partners who are tempted to push for their own way. When you push, the other will push back. So if you don't want stubborn resistance, use motivation and compromise rather than force.

Here are some additional pointers:

- When you need help, rather than expecting immediate compliance, give your spouse a warning, or ask when it would be convenient to help.
- Time your request so your spouse is not deeply absorbed in an important activity.
- Ask for cooperation, rather than telling.
- Give a reason without getting defensive.
- Be willing to cheerfully work along with him or her—rather than making your spouse work alone or you sitting on the sidelines giving advice.

"Let nothing be done through selfish ambition or conceit, but in lowliness of mind let each esteem others better than himself." —Philippians 2:3, NKJV

Avoiding Family Feuds

Marriage doesn't just bring two people with different personalities together; it brings two extended families together. And as every married couple knows, not all the relatives are easy to get along with. But that doesn't mean you shouldn't try, because it's easier to have a good marriage when you're not fighting with the extended family.

Here's the secret: Members of families who are able to retain close relationships are those who respect each other and feel good enough about themselves that they hold no grudges.

A relationship takes two people. And in some relationships, because of different personalities, it takes considerably more time and effort to make the relationship work than in others.

A 1990 Harris poll found that 97 percent of Americans said that a happy family was their top priority, while only 60 percent said a good income was. Why, then, is so much more time invested in earning money than in earning and maintaining the love and respect of all the family members?

"Behold, how good and how pleasant it is for brethren to dwell together in unity!" —Psalm 133:1, NKJV

DR. KAY KUZMA

Treat Your Husband Like a Dog

When I got engaged, one of my friends gave me a dog training book and crossed out all the references to a dog and replaced them with the word "husband." It was a joke; but the more I read, the more I realized there was some truth in that book!

Have you ever trained a dog? They're eager to please and will do all sorts of unnatural things, like playing dead, singing, or shaking hands, because they know they will be rewarded. Men (and women, I might add) aren't so different. We all like to please and when we know that our actions will bring a smile or a compliment, we tend to repeat them.

Yet, many wives, without thinking, give more attention to their husband's faults. And the result? They reinforce the very things they don't like!

So, begin noticing the positive. Let him overhear you telling someone else something nice about him. And give him plenty of nonverbal positive strokes like a hug, a wink, or a smile.

Husbands, like dogs, will repeat those things that get attention, so make sure you give it when he's doing something that pleases you.

"Rejoice and be exceedingly glad, for great is your reward in heaven." —Matthew 5:12, NKJV

Two Keys to Self-Value

If you want to preserve and build each other's sense of personal value, you must make sure your mate feels both *desirable* and *competent*.

Sometimes very capable people feel incompetent. They may struggle with something new or complicated, make a costly mistake, forget something important, or default to an old addiction—and those ugly feelings of "I can't do anything right," come rushing in to destroy the sense of competence.

Compliments and encouragement are good competence boosters and married couples should give them out liberally, but there's something else that works even better to make sure your mate maintains a sense of personal value. It's making sure your loved one feels desirable, wanted, and cherished—regardless of how competent he or she feels at the moment.

Your mate will feel desirable when you make it clear you love to be close, you enjoy touching, and your body language says he or she is important to you. The number one job of married couples is to make their partner feels *desirable,* because when a person doesn't, he or she is easy prey to feelings of inferiority and incompetence.

"Therefore be merciful, just as your Father also is merciful." —Luke 6:36, NKJV

DR. KAY KUZMA

The Window of Your Soul

Just like eye contact is critical for parents bonding with infants, it's critical for the development of a healthy marriage relationship! In fact, sight is one of the senses that you used most when falling in love. Remember how you gazed into each other's eyes? Remember the playful, teasing glances and the lingering "I just can't get enough of you" kind of looks you gave each other?

But unfortunately, one of the first things busy couples give up when they get married is eye-to-eye contact because they get too busy. When each is looking at the other, it's difficult to do anything else, so it's more meaningful. That's why it's such a strong bonding activity.

Eyes are the windows to one's soul. When you are really focusing on each other, gazing into your spouse's eyes, you get to know the inner dimension of a person. You perceive emotion, depth of character, spirituality, the essence of who your mate is—which is the precursor of profound intimacy.

Take the time to really look at each other and strengthen your bond for life.

"Look upon me and be merciful to me, as Your custom is toward those who love Your name."
—Psalm 119:132, NKJV

A Riddle of Love

Do you enjoy riddles? Remember the one about what's black and white and "red" all over? The answer: A newspaper. But here's another that isn't as well known, but should be because it is the key to having a vibrant marriage. *What's the only thing you can give away and end up with more?*

The answer is LOVE. That's right. If you fill up your mate so full of love that he or she can't seem to contain it, the chances are great that something nice will come back to you.

Love is fairly abstract, but it becomes more concrete when you think of people as having love cups, which either empty or fill depending upon what happens to them. The substance that fills a love cup is attention—positive attention. The more you give, the more you get.

Remember this riddle when you're feeling a little lonely, when your life together seems boring, and you don't have time for each other. Take the time to be a love cup filler—and enjoy the drops of joy that splash back on you.

"Beloved, let us love one another, for love is of God; and everyone who loves is born of God and knows God."
—1 John 4:7, NKJV

DR. KAY KUZMA

Immunize Each Other Against the Negative

Negative attitudes are contagious! Your boss complains about something at work, your co-workers complain about the boss, you come home and complain to your mate about your job—and then you wonder why you're both so grumpy.

If you're not careful a negative attitude can make life miserable for everyone you come in contact with!

Negative attitudes zap your energy. Just work next to someone who only sees the negative side of life and is always complaining and criticizing, and I'll guarantee you'll be more tired at the end of the day than if you work next to an optimistic person.

You can't always change your work environment, but you can protect yourself and your mate from catching negative attitudes. Just make sure you immunize each other the first thing in the morning with a prayer of thanksgiving, a word of encouragement, and a meaningful hug and kiss.

"I will bless the LORD at all times; His praise shall continually be in my mouth." —Psalm 34:1, NKJV

Don't Be Afraid of Silence

Have you ever tried to have a phone conversation with the TV blaring, the kids screaming, the dog barking, and your spouse trying to get the vacuuming done.

It's interesting how often we require silence when we're talking to a stranger on the phone, and yet in our own homes when we're talking to the people who mean the most to us, we don't even think about turning off the radio or TV, stopping what we're doing, looking them in the eyes—and really listening. Is it any wonder so little real communication goes on within families?

It's almost as if we're afraid of silence. Without thinking we get in the car and flip on the radio. Or we come through the back door and turn on the TV. Or we tune out the family noise by attaching a Bluetooth to our ear and we listen to our MP3 player, rather than each other.

Let me challenge you to live one week without radio, TV or computer sounds! If you do, I have a feeling that you may fill the silence with meaningful conversations and your marriage should be better for it.

"Be still, and know that I am God." —Psalm 46:10, NKJV

DR. KAY KUZMA

Opposites Attract

Have you ever wondered if it would be best to marry someone who has a different personality type than your own?

Well, the chances are great that you married your opposite, because opposites attract. People tend to look for someone who will be complementary to them. If you are weak in one area, you will be drawn toward someone who is strong.

But just because opposites attract, it doesn't mean opposites necessarily get along! Those very traits that you find so attractive during courtship can become abrasive after marriage, because the person values, thinks, and does things differently than you.

So, regardless of whom you marry, the important thing to remember is that your mate *will* have personality differences you are going to have to learn to accept and appreciate. Marry because you love the person's faults—not his or her strengths. And once married, daily renew your commitment to love, in spite of the faults!

"Oh, how great are God's riches and wisdom and knowledge! How impossible it is for us to understand his decisions and his ways!" —Romans 11:33, NLT

Beat the Bad Weather Blahs

Just because it's stormy outside, doesn't mean you have to put up with stormy relationships inside. A little creativity can transform winter blahs into a blast.

There had been a blustering, cold wind blowing all weekend and the roads were icy. By Sunday afternoon, Trent and Paula and their kids were tired of being cooped up and were irritable and short-tempered. "I wish we could get out of this house and do something fun," complained Paula.

"Fun" to Trent, meant romantic. He sent Paula upstairs with a book and then called the neighbors to care for the kids. He quickly put together a picnic basket full of goodies, spread a blanket on the floor, put on their favorite CD, lowered the lights, and lit some candles. An hour later, he and Paula were sitting beside a roaring fire and enjoyed telling each other stories from their childhoods and recalling the best memories from their marriage.

You can beat the blahs with a little creativity: Put together a puzzle; look through your old photo albums; write love letters to each other and exchange them.

Beat the bad weather blahs—don't let them beat you!

"And whatever you do, do it heartily, as to the Lord and not to men." —Colossians 3:23, NKJV

DR. KAY KUZMA

When Your Mate Is a Workaholic

A wife once commented, "I have a lot of anger and frustration harbored toward my husband. He's a workaholic. Often I feel used, unloved, and burdened with domestic responsibility. And the children feel rejected when he says he's too busy to do things with them. Sometimes I feel like just packing up and leaving."

I responded, "That's not a bad idea!"

You're probably shocked by what sounds like a cold-hearted response, when I've dedicated my life to keeping families together. The problem is addiction. When someone is addicted to drugs, alcohol—or work—the worst thing you can do is cover for him or her and allow the person to continue in his or her destructive patterns.

You must do something to get the person's attention, to let him know you and the children are hurting, and that he must make a choice. Your workaholic mate must be confronted with the consequences of his addiction, which hopefully will give him enough motivation to change. And just to set the record straight: men aren't the only ones who can become addicted to work!

"And if it seems evil to you to serve the LORD, choose for yourselves this day whom you will serve."
—Joshua 24:15, NKJV

Some Mates Have to See to Understand

Katie had tried talking to her husband, but was having trouble getting him to understand how she felt when she tried to share her feelings and he dismissed them as unimportant. Finally, she got her point across when she described how she felt in graphic terms.

She said, "I feel like a big slug crawling slowly along the pavement, trying to get out of the way of your big feet. And when you see me (the slug) struggling, you pour salt on me, causing me to disintegrate before your eyes." She ended her word picture with, "That's how I feel every time I try to say something about how I'm feeling and you interrupt me, laugh at me, or put me down for being so sensitive. I'm just a slug and you're killing me."

He got the picture, and tears came to his eyes when he realized what he had been doing to her.

If you're having trouble getting your mate to understand why you feel the way you do, take time to paint a word picture, and see if it doesn't make a difference. Some people just have to see to understand.

"And be kind to one another, tenderhearted, forgiving one another, even as God in Christ forgave you."
—Ephesians 4:32, NKJV

DR. KAY KUZMA

Marriage Is No Place for Tantrums

Have you ever seen an adult throw a temper tantrum? It's pretty scary, isn't it? Kids throw tantrums because they don't have the verbal skills to put their feelings into words. But as children learn to express how they feel, their tantrums decrease. If you can communicate your feelings in words, there is no need to throw a tantrum.

Why then do so many husbands and wives impulsively act out their angry feelings instead of talk them out? It's because they have never learned how to appropriately deal with them.

Here's what they should do: First, consider why they are having these negative feelings. Acknowledge that something is wrong. The faster people can right the wrong or work out their feelings, the better. If angry feelings aren't dealt with, they will likely get more ugly and troublesome and marriage partners will act them out by hurting their spouse and others.

If you've never learned how to talk out or work out negative feelings, join an anger management class or your tantrums could end up threatening your marriage.

"Wrath is cruel and anger a torrent. . . .Open rebuke is better than love carefully concealed."
—Proverbs 27:4, 5, NKJV

Try, Try Again

When you are tempted to give up on your marriage, here's a little poem by T. C. Hamlet that might encourage you to keep trying.

Two frogs fell into a can of cream, or so I've heard it told;
The sides of the can were shiny and steep, the cream was deep and cold.
"O, what's the use?" croaked No. 1. " 'Tis fate; no help's around.
Goodbye, my friends! Goodbye, sad world!" And weeping still, he drowned.
But Number 2, of sterner stuff, dog-paddled in surprise,
The while he wiped his creamy face and dried his creamy eyes.
"I'll swim awhile, at least," he said—or so I've heard it said;
"It really wouldn't help the world, if one more frog were dead."
An hour or two he kicked and swam, not once he stopped to mutter,
But kicked and kicked and swam and kicked, then hopped out, via butter!

I can't promise that trying again will heal a broken marriage, or that you can hop out of your problems via butter; but at the same time, far too many hurting marriages could be saved if each of the partners would just try a little harder!

"A desire accomplished is sweet to the soul." —Proverbs 13:19, NKJV

DR. KAY KUZMA

Peace at Home

A husband complained, "My wife and children argue all the time. From the moment I walk into the house until the kids are in bed, a battle is going on somewhere. When I try to solve the problem, it only seems to make things worse. I'm beginning to dread coming home. All I want is a little peace and quiet!"

Many men feel this way. When they got married, they expected their homes would be peaceful havens away from the hustle and bustle of the world; and now with a couple of children, and wives who desperately needs vacations, they find themselves living in war zones!

Instead of escaping to the office—or to the Bahamas—or filing for divorce, husbands need to take an active role in the family. Call a family council. Work together on establishing some battle free times and zones, and in between, practice some problem-solving skills.

There is never a time when a family needs loving leadership more then when they are at war. Now is not the time to withdraw!

"Depart from evil and do good; seek peace and pursue it." —Psalm 34:14, NKJV

Marriage Goals

What do you want out of marriage? Great sex? Financial security? Romance? Companionship? A stronger spiritual life? Acceptance? Recognition?

When I wrote down my answers, I found them rather selfish. Maybe that's because when it comes to marriage, asking what we want is the wrong question.

Perhaps we should be asking something more along the lines of President John F. Kennedy's famous words: "Ask not what your country can do for you, but what you can do for your country." Or applying this to marriage: "Ask not what your marriage can do for you, but what you can do for your marriage."

Here is how I answered this question:

1. To uplift my husband and help him become everything God created him to be.
2. To be a loyal companion, a loving sex partner, and a positive influence on the most wonderful man in my world.
3. To encourage and contribute to my husband's spiritual growth and personal fulfillment.

Now it's your turn: What can you give to your marriage?

"And what does the Lord require of you but to do justly, to love mercy, and to walk humbly with your God?"
—Micah 6:8, NKJV

DR. KAY KUZMA

Overworked and Accomplishing Little

I love finding words of wisdom that can help me be a better wife. For example, "Better one handful with tranquility than two handfuls with toil and chasing after the wind."

Wow! That hit home! I thought about all the times I rushed to get to that extra appointment to make a little more money. Or the times I told my husband, "I'm too busy," because I couldn't say No to someone else! Or when I tried multitasking, and got started on too many projects and finished nothing!

Is your life filled with toil and you seem to be chasing after the wind? In other words, are you overworked but don't seem to be getting much done? If so, maybe you're trying to do too much. Overwork causes frustration and burnout. It can also cause family resentment and alienation.

Maybe you ought to reconsider and be content with one handful, rather than two!

"Better one handful with tranquility than two handfuls with toil and chasing after the wind." —Ecclesiastes 4:6, NIV

Sexual Desire

Your sexual desire is dependent on many things. For men, it can be triggered by a look. For women, it's usually the little acts of kindness throughout the day that make her heat up. It's kind of like the difference between instantly nuking your food with a microwave versus simmering it on the stove. One of the most challenging lessons a couple can learn is how to lovingly arouse each other so sex is a mutually satisfying experience.

But sexual desire is more complicated than just understanding gender differences. It can be affected by what has happened in the past, hormones, stress, age, and pain. If any of this is happening in your marriage, get professional help to overcome these obstacles because 1 Corinthians 7:2–5 makes it clear that husbands and wives should not withhold themselves from each other—unless for a short, agreed upon time.

It's magic when a couple's sexual needs and desires are so similar that each gives generously and unselfishly to meet the other's needs. That's God's ideal for you.

"The husband should fulfill his wife's sexual needs, and the wife should fulfill her husband's needs."
—1 Corinthians 7:3, NLT

DR. KAY KUZMA

Constructive Criticism

You've heard the term "constructive criticism," but I bet you've seldom gotten it. Criticism is criticism, and it almost always hurts. But at the same time, there are times when a mate needs to know how his or her behavior is affecting you so changes can be made—or so he or she isn't embarrassed by someone else's criticism.

The art of being a good marriage partner is to correct without criticism. The best way to do this is to sandwich your correction between words of appreciation. Start with something positive, "I appreciate you helping me set the table for guests; just remember next time to put the knife on the right side and the fork on the left." And then you might want to add, "And by the way, the centerpiece looks great."

Here's another suggestion, correct in private. This is especially important when you have children around. If you don't sandwich your correction of your mate with words of love, it sounds as if you're being disrespectful, and the chances are great that the kids will copy you!

"Let your speech always be with grace, seasoned with salt, that you may know how you ought to answer each one."
—Colossians 4:6, NKJV

What Wives Want From Men!

I once wrote an article where I said that the biggest fault of men was not paying enough attention to their wives. I got an interesting response from a woman who said, "I don't agree. My husband showers me with flowers and candy, and then kills me with put-downs. Please don't encourage the showy expressions of love, without talking about things like showing an accepting attitude and saying kind words. Teach men that gentle touches throughout the day, plus comments that show how much they value their wives, is what women need most."

Well said, don't you think? Just paying attention to your mate is not enough. It's the quality of the attention. And you can't build your mate up with a gift one moment and tear her down the next. A very talented girl was once asked what she saw in the fellow she was marrying. Her response was, "He treats me with respect and values me supremely!"

Men, I hope you take note. You may think you're giving your wife what she needs, but if it's not an abundant amount of love and respect—and NO put-downs—then you're not giving her what she wants!

"We love Him because He first loved us." —1 John 4:19, NKJV

DR. KAY KUZMA

Couple Ministry for the Rejected

Are you looking for a ministry you can do with your spouse? Think about encouraging friends who are suffering from the rejection of separation or divorce.

There is no experience, other than death, that is so devastating to a person than divorce. Yet many find themselves not only divorced from their spouses, but divorced from their friends as well. One reason is because of the perception that the divorced single is on the lookout for a spouse, and therefore a potential threat to the marriages of others. Another reason that married couples state is that since both of the divorced were friends, to speak to one would offend the other.

Don't reject your divorced friends. As a couple, let your ministry be to encourage them. Let them know that you still accept them as individuals. Invite them to be a part of your family. Take time to listen. Don't try to counsel or act as a go-between. Be friends to both parties. Your friends need you.

"I want them to be encouraged and knit together by strong ties of love. I want them to have complete confidence that they understand God's mysterious plan, which is Christ himself." —Colossians 2:2, NLT

How to Listen With Love

Too often we think of talking as the way to be actively involved in a conversation. But if you listen right, listening can be active. In fact, it might just be that listening can be the best way to get the "I love you" message across to your mate.

Lean forward, look interested, and don't be afraid of periods of silence. It will give your spouse a chance to think, and hopefully, he or she will make the next response. Caution! If silence makes you feel uncomfortable and you think you need to fill up every moment of the conversation, you'll end up controlling it.

Then respond appropriately, sharing your own ideas when it will help to further your mutual understanding.

It takes time and work to listen actively. But it's the only kind of listening that will give the "I love you" message.

"He who answers a matter before he hears it, it is folly and shame to him." —Proverbs 18:13, NKJV

Who Is the Real Leader?

You've heard the joke that although the man is the head of the family, his wife is the neck that turns the head. Who IS the real leader of your family?

I have a feeling most men would identify with the cartoon I saw the other day that pictured a frustrated person frantically looking around, asking, "Which way did they go? How many of them were there? How fast were they going? I MUST find them; I am their LEADER!"

If you feel your family is leaving you behind, maybe it's time to re-evaluate your leadership skills. First of all, a leader gets involved. A leader has a vision for the family, communicating how to reach the goals, and helping when needed. A leader listens to the concerns of others and knows how to lift up and encourage.

Any woman married to a man with those kind of leadership skills isn't going to want to be the neck. She's going to be perfectly satisfied to stand beside him and be the helpmate God created her to be.

"For the husband is head of the wife, as also Christ is head of the church." —Ephesians 5:23, NKJV

Cleave and Leave

Don't let your marriage be destroyed by a meddling mother, an overbearing father, or an opinionated grandpare There's wisdom in the biblical advice to cleave to your wife or husband and leave your family of origin. In toda world, that means, don't live with your parents—or even close to your parents—if they can't keep their mouths shi

Husbands and wives shouldn't have to compete with the in-laws for their spouses' attention. Mothers and fathe shouldn't meddle. Parents don't have to know everything about their son's or daughter's lives once they are marrie And they don't have to give their opinions, unless asked.

Too many grown kids remain tied to their parents' apron strings after they are married. Here's the fact. You ca grow closer to your mate, unless you let go of your mom and dad. You don't have to hurt them or totally ignore the but just as good fences make good neighbors, good boundaries between a married couple and their families of origi make good marriages.

"Therefore shall a man leave his father and his mother, and shall cleave unto his wife: and they shall be one flesh." —Genesis 2:24, KJV

Every Marriage Needs Irrational Love

*I*rrational isn't usually something good. But it's essential in a good marriage. It gives your mate the security of knowing that your love is not based on his or her actions. You don't love your mate because he's dependable or because she's pretty. In fact, there is no reason for your love, other than the fact that this person exists and you are committed to love and respect him or her for life.

When marriage partners know that they are loved irrationally—or you might say, unconditionally—it frees them to be who they really are. They don't have to act a certain way to get your love or to keep your love.

Without irrational love, a marriage partner feels like a puppet on a string, doing whatever the mate wants in order to be loved. One partner is constantly being controlled by the whims of the other. Your wife pulls the strings and you react in a certain way to make sure you please her so you won't get punished by withholding sex. Your husband pulls the strings and you give in to his demands because you are afraid he will criticize you if you don't.

So when it comes to love, let it be irrational! And the more irrational the better!

"For God so loved the world that He gave His only begotten Son." —John 3:16, NKJV

Let Thanks Be Served for Supper

The best way I've found to have a joyful heart is to choose to be thankful and to let people know how much I appreciate them. I try to do this regardless of their motives, or whether or not I've tipped them or they have in some other way been paid for their kindness.

You can't change your spouse or make your kids happier individuals, but you can change yourself. Stop taking the kindness and good deeds of others for granted. Increase the number of times you say "Thank you" throughout the day. Let your children hear your words of thanks. Give away words of appreciation liberally to your spouse, and I doubt if he or she will complain.

Finally, don't be afraid to ask for words of appreciation for yourself. Say something like, "Did you like supper? If so, the cook would love to hear a word of thanks—or you could leave a generous tip—whichever you'd prefer!"

"O Lord my God, I will give thanks to You forever." —Psalm 30:12, NKJV

DR. KAY KUZMA

Don't Feed the Monkeys

Do you have too much on your plate and you find yourself doing everything else except spending meaningful time with the person you love most? Think of all those things that are vying for your attention as monkeys. Then remember this truism: If you feed a monkey, it will attach itself to you and demand your attention.

If it is someone else's job or idea, let him or her figure out how the monkey is going to get taken care of. Never say "Yes," to a request from someone unless you sleep on it, pray about it, and consult your mate. Be willing to say, "I'd love to, but it's not my monkey."

Be careful to not let monkeys get into your house. They are especially skilled at sneaking in with the mail, Internet, or the phone!

And don't start your weekend with a cage full of monkeys. Everyone, especially busy couples, needs a weekly day of rest. Plan your schedule in such a way as to get everything done on weekdays, and leave the weekends free for each other. Your mate will love and respect you more if you put him or her first, rather than the monkeys in your life.

"Better is a handful with quietness than both hands full, together with toil and grasping for the wind."
—Ecclesiastes 4:6, NKJV

Who Should Make What Decision?

How should a couple go about making decisions? Who should have the final word? Should everything be decided together?

Obviously, no two people agree on everything, but the best marriages are those where couples compromise—and sometimes agree to disagree, allowing the person who will be affected the most by the decision to make the final call.

The important thing is that the issue is thoroughly discussed; the pros and cons considered; and each is willing to stretch to accommodate the needs, values, and wants of the other.

Here's the key to good decision-making: If the person who feels strongest about the decision, will in love choose to accommodate most to the other, a couple will have very few conflicts. It all boils down to trust and respect and a whole lot of unselfishness.

The important thing is that neither one takes advantage of the other by making big decisions on his or her own. Once that happens, it's really hard to trust!

"Please let there be no strife between you and me . . . for we are brethren." —Genesis 13:8, NKJV

DR. KAY KUZMA

Gifts Wives Like Most

Wives enjoy having their husbands bring them special gifts. Yet it's not the gift that wins a woman, it's what the gift signifies. It makes her feel special. When you remember her birthday, she feels like somebody. When you show her little attentions, she knows you're thinking about her. And when you bring her something for no reason at all, she knows she is loved unconditionally.

But, too many men use gifts to get something, like sex or permission to go hunting with the guys. They think a gift will buy their wives' approval. Sometimes gifts are used to atone for mistakes, like when men crucify their wives with painful words or actions and then hope a big enough gift will buy her forgiveness.

Wives want love gifts, but they don't want things as much as they want respect, consideration, and thoughtfulness. For a woman those are the best gifts of all.

"He will accept no recompense, nor will he be appeased though you give many gifts." —Proverbs 6:35, NKJV

Have You Burnt the Ships?

Elsa Einstein, the wife of the intellectual giant that gave the world the theory of relativity, was once asked if she understood it. "No," she replied, "I don't understand my husband's theory of relativity, but I know my husband and I know he can be trusted." There is no greater compliment that Elsa could have given her husband.

Marriage is built on trust—and grows on trust. When you say "I do," you have no idea what lies ahead, so the commitment you make to each other is only as strong as you are trustworthy. Did you really mean what you said when you vowed, "Until death do us part"?

The secret to making your marriage commitment work is to never look back. Instead you and your mate must do as Hernando Cortés, the Spanish conqueror did when he landed in Mexico in 1519. Fearing his men might consider retreat if things got tough, he ordered the ships to be burnt.

To burn the ships means divorce is NOT an option, but it doesn't need to be because nothing can break up your marriage if both of you are totally committed to each other—and trustworthy.

"Commit everything you do to the LORD. Trust him, and he will help you." —Psalm 37:5, NLT

DR. KAY KUZMA

Avoid Uncontrolled Anger

If your impulsive displays of anger have gotten you into trouble and your mate is avoiding you, you need a quick lesson in how to win friends, influence people, and keep a spouse. And angry outbursts don't! Here are three points to remember:

1. State how you feel without making the other person feel he or she is responsible. Usually anger is the end product of hurt, disappointment, or other milder emotions. Speak up at those levels and you'll avoid a lot of anger.
2. If you mouth off and hurt your loved one, apologize, even if you think you're right.
3. If your anger is a result of your mate trying to change you, take the initiative. Ask for specific suggestions on how you can improve.

Whether you follow these points or not is your decision, but it will clarify your mate's expectations so you will know where you stand.

Here's an example, "I feel hurt when I'm treated like this. I'm sorry I offended you. Let me know what you expect of me. Our relationship is the most important thing in my life."

"But You are God, ready to pardon, gracious and merciful, slow to anger, abundant in kindness, and did not forsake them." —Nehemiah 9:17, NKJV

Should Moms Work?

Does your husband disapprove of the fact that you're working outside the home while the children are still at home? If he does, and you enjoy having a job, make a pact to be honest, open-minded, and respectful of each other. Then try this exercise.

Make a list of the negative and positive aspects of your job. Be specific. Ask your husband to do the same. Then compare the two lists. Look at the positive side first, and try to agree on as many positive points as possible.

Then compare the negative side. Brainstorm possible solutions for each negative point. Quitting would be one answer. Continuing to work without any changes would be the opposite. Be willing to compromise. Consider some of these ideas: part-time work; hire a housekeeper; fix meals ahead of time; arrange a more flexible work schedule; move closer to the job; or come home promptly after work.

With compromise and creativity you can work out a solution about work.

"Listen to counsel and receive instruction, that you may be wise in your latter days." —Proverbs 19:20, NKJV

DR. KAY KUZMA

Time for High-Level Communication

Most of the time we communicate in *clichés*. Without thinking we say, "Hi, how are you?" "Nice day, isn't it?" But if mere chitchat is the main substance of communication between husbands and wives, then there isn't much satisfaction.

How much better to at least *report* things that have happened to you or share facts that you have heard. Your mate can't argue with a report, unless it's reported inaccurately. You show you're interested in each other by reporting something you think the other would like to hear—or needs to hear.

But you'll learn more about each other if you'll talk about your *ideas and opinions,* which is the next higher level of communication. There is a risk involved that the other person will think differently about certain issues. But along with the risk there is the added satisfaction of sharing what is on your heart.

But don't stop there. Real closeness comes when you share your *feelings.*

"Give ear to my prayer, O God, and do not hide Yourself from my supplication." —Psalm 55:1, NKJV

Romance Is a Relationship

No matter how many anniversaries have passed, you can still add the sparkle of romance to your relationship. Romance doesn't require money, despite the fact that the media hints that wining and dining or French perfume and diamonds are the magic formula to entice your lover. But it does take time.

What is romance? It's a tendency toward the wonderful or the mysterious; anticipation, suspense, planning, imagination, humor. It's achieved by thinking of special and unique ways of saying, "I love you," by getting away from that dull routine, and by celebrating little rituals. It flourishes when you feel free to be yourself and are willing to be vulnerable to the one to whom you have committed your life.

Choosing to romance each other in creative ways during love play brings heightened sensations. Break the routine; flirt; nothing that pleases both is off-limits for married couples.

Simply stated, romance is sharing. It's sharing precious moments as you care for each other's needs and wishes. Romance is a relationship. Make yours the best ever!

"Let him kiss me with the kisses of his mouth—for your love is better than wine." —Song of Solomon 1:2, NKJV

DR. KAY KUZMA

The Myths of Marriage

It's frustrating to believe a lie and then discover that you've been duped. Well, it's time to discover the truth about three marriage myths.

Myth 1: *Marriages are happier when men and women follow expected gender roles.* Not so. Marriages where both husband and wife carry their fair share of work and home responsibilities are far happier than marriages where a husband might say, "I'd never clean the bathroom—that's a woman's job," or a wife comments, "I might know more about finances, but I expect my husband to take that responsibility since he's the head of the family."

Myth 2: *Marriage is hard work.* Not so. Work implies something unpleasant that you must do to get what you want. When couples love each other supremely and are committed to the other's best interest, the element of play, rather than work, is the magic that makes great relationships.

Myth 3: *Marriages with children are more satisfying.* Not so. Couples with kids are more committed to their marriages, but not necessarily more satisfied. Knowing this, what can you do to defy the odds and make your marriage the best ever?

"Lead me in Your truth and teach me, for You are the God of my salvation; on You I wait all the day."
—Psalm 25:5, NKJV

How to Beat the Heat

Here's a great list of "keep cool" ideas for marriages.

1. Refresh your mind by reading something uplifting.
2. Face the billowy breeze of life's frustrations by flying a kite.
3. Shower yourself by counting your blessings.
4. Drink in the affirmations of others.
5. Keep cool and calm in the middle of an argument.
6. When you receive lemons, make lemonade.
7. Break the ice with someone against whom you are holding a grudge.
8. Create a pleasant "air-conditioned" climate in your home.
9. Splash joy into the life of your spouse.
10. Swim continually in God's love.

Regardless of the outside temperature, you can beat the heat by replacing your frustration and worry with thankfulness and celebration.

"Be anxious for nothing, but in everything by prayer and supplication, with thanksgiving,
let your requests be made known to God." —Philippians 4:6, NKJV

DR. KAY KUZMA

Greener Pastures in Your Own Backyard

The grass always seems greener on the other side of the fence, doesn't it? Many wives who work would rather be home, while many others would love a job!

If you're home, yet somehow don't feel as fulfilled as you thought you would when you quit your job, chances are you're not missing the hectic schedule! You're missing the satisfaction of knowing you did a job well, contributed something to this world, and received the appreciation of others.

You've got to discover how to get these same things from your time at home without taking advantage of your spouse. It's unfair to expect him to meet all your emotional needs.

You must plan ways to find satisfaction at home. Some wives enjoy crafts; others volunteer. What's your training or skills? Use them. Or learn a new skill. What you get out of life is what you put into it! It's your responsibility to make sure the grass on your side of the fence is the greenest of all!

"Oh, satisfy us early with Your mercy, that we may rejoice and be glad all our days!" —Psalm 90:14, NKJV

Busting the Blues

Have you ever felt like saying, "I'm just going to go eat worms!" Of course, worms won't help get you out of the dumps. And you shouldn't expect your mate to make you happy. So take responsibility for yourself. You can do something about the occasional blues!

- Take time to contact a family member or friend who makes you feel warm inside. If no one comes to mind, you may need to enlarge your circle of friends.
- Force yourself to reach out and do something nice for someone. Start with your mate.
- Read or listen to something uplifting. Search for Bible promises or listen to uplifting music.
- Get some exercise. A long walk in the fresh air will do wonders.
- Put your house or apartment in order. A messy place can be depressing.
- Start planning something that you've always wanted to do. Write down your dream and develop a plan of action that will lead to fulfillment. Then get started.

Your mate will find you a lot more attractive when you're living your dream then when you're "eating worms"!

"Delight yourself also in the Lord, and He shall give you the desires of your heart." —Psalm 37:4, NKJV

DR. KAY KUZMA

Warm Fuzzies and Cold Pricklies

Everyone needs warm fuzzies to feel valuable and loved—like compliments, words of affirmation, and all those nice little things people do for you.

However, no one likes cold pricklies—words of criticism, sarcastic looks, and things that make you feel rejected and persecuted.

Yet some people have a hard time giving away warm fuzzies—and that person may be your husband or your wife. Without thinking he or she may say and do things that hurt you.

Receiving a few cold pricklies won't freeze you to death. But if you're getting a lot more cold pricklies than warm fuzzies and your spouse just can't seem to break the cold prickly habit, you need to broaden your same gender friendship base.

Smile often. Speak to those who look more uncomfortable than you feel. There is a warm fuzzy friend out there somewhere who will give you the positive attention you need so you can keep giving warm fuzzies to your cold prickly spouse.

"Wait on the LORD; be of good courage, and He shall strengthen your heart; wait, I say, on the LORD!"
—Psalm 27:14, NKJV

Is Your Mate a TV-aholic?

Have you heard the saying, you can lead a horse to water, but you can't make him drink? Well, that's the way it is trying to pry some people away from the TV!

Your spouse may not be a TV-aholic who habitually watches everything that comes on, but he or she might binge at times, sitting there glued to the evening news or the sports channel, oblivious to your needs.

If you'd like to start breaking that TV habit, maybe you need to be more fun to be with. Each day schedule some time together, at least fifteen to thirty minutes. Plan interesting things to do: A bike ride around the block; a wiener roast in the fireplace; a candid camera plot.

If nothing else, record his favorite programs so he can watch them when you have time to cuddle up together and enjoy the TV—and each other.

"All the ways of a man are pure in his own eyes, but the Lord weighs the spirits." —Proverbs 16:2, NKJV

DR. KAY KUZMA

Finding Your Marriage Mission

One of the greatest gifts you and your mate can give each other is the joy you'll get when working together for the Lord. Every person needs a mission: a dream, a calling, a special task that he or she would do regardless of the pay. And every marriage needs a mission, something that will bring you closer together—something beyond your daily routine. Something that will bless others and make this world a better place.

Helping street people is one idea—or you might go on a building trip. Maybe with Habitat for Humanity to build houses in Nepal or on a Maranatha project to build churches and schools in India or Africa.

Start your search close to home. Is there a neighbor you can help by painting a room or fixing up the yard? Is there a child you could babysit and give the child's folks a much needed day off? Check your community for service projects and get involved.

If you're looking for something that will focus your energy and enthusiasm on others while at the same time bring you closer together, you need a marriage mission.

"When God's people are in need, be ready to help them. Always be eager to practice hospitality." —Romans 12:13, NLT

Husbands Are Like Strings

Do you sometimes find your husband resisting your suggestions or pleas for help? It may be because he feels you are trying to control him and force him to do something he doesn't want to do.

Here's the problem: Husbands are very much like strings. If you stretch a string out straight and push one end of the string in the direction you want it to go, it will buckle under the pressure of being pushed. Husbands when pushed, forced, and manipulated will tend to resist. Instead, take the other end of the string and lead the string in the direction you want it to go, and it will follow.

So instead of pushing or forcing your husband to do something he doesn't want to do, motivate, encourage, influence, and lead him in the right direction. When you do, you'll both end up winning!

"The LORD is my shepherd. . . . He leads me beside the still waters. He restores my soul;
He leads me in paths of righteousness for His name's sake." —Psalm 23:1–3, NKJV

DR. KAY KUZMA

Give Your Spouse What Is Needed

If you've picked up the erroneous idea that your marriage partner should be treated as he deserves to be treated, you've probably discovered the painful fact that "fairness" doesn't build healthy relationships.

Being an effective marriage partner means meeting your mate's needs, and a person's greatest need is to be loved unconditionally—regardless of what he or she does or what he or she deserves—or what you may consider fair. In addition, your mate also needs good companionship, healthy respect, a positive atmosphere, and a whole lot of forgiveness. That's how you build a marriage.

Divorce courts are full of couples who tried to operate their marriages on fairness. If he gets a new car, I deserve one. If she goes out with her girlfriends, I should be able to go out with the guys. If he criticizes me, I'll criticize him. If he comes home late, he can just fix his own dinner. If she won't forgive, why should I? Try treating your spouse as you think he or she deserves and your marriage is heading for disaster! Instead, meet each other's needs.

"There is a way that seems right to a man, but its end is the way of death." —Proverbs 16:25, NKJV

Radical Tongue Surgery

If your relationship is sometimes rocky and you desperately want to put things back together again, but every time you try to say something your spouse detects a hidden agenda and runs the other way, the situation calls for radical tongue surgery!

You must cut away all instructive communication that makes your spouse think you would like to change him or her, like, "Honey, if you would only . . ." In fact, strike "if you" from your vocabulary. And watch your tone of voice. No one wants to be married to a drill sergeant.

Next cut out the "why," "what," "where," "when," "who," and "did" questions. If you wonder why, count the number of questions lawyers ask when they are interrogating the accused. If you take the offensive by asking a question, it will put your husband or wife on the defensive and you can expect your mate to fight back.

And finally, cut out all criticism, gossip, and complaining. Substitute words of encouragement, praise, and appreciation.

"Whoso offereth praise glorifieth me: and to him that ordereth his conversation aright will I shew the salvation of God."
—Psalm 50:23, KJV

DR. KAY KUZMA

Where Is Your Marriage Heading?

Have you taken time recently to consider where your marriage is heading? What has been the trend of your life together these last few months? And if you continue this trend, do you like where you're likely to end up?

It's easy to float downstream. And that's what most of us do in marriage. We merely get up in the morning, brush our teeth, and let the day sweep us away.

Let me suggest another approach. If you could live one ideal day, what would you want to be doing and where? Maybe it is doing something special for your mate or spending time together walking on the beach or sharing good food and conversation together with another couple. Whatever it is, the chances of you ever living that perfect day is pretty small, unless you start planning for it now.

Start by putting a piece of your ideal day into each day. Maybe it's only thirty minutes out of twenty-four hours. Just don't put off living until tomorrow, because tomorrow may never come.

"I know that nothing is better for them than to rejoice, and to do good in their lives, and also that every man should eat and drink and enjoy the good of all his labor—it is the gift of God." —Ecclesiastes 3:12, 13, NKJV

When Your Spouse Makes You Mad

There are three ways to deal with your negative emotions: Act them out, work them out, or talk them out. Talking is by far the most preferred method of removal: Talk to God, talk to your mate, talk to a counselor, or write them down.

If negative emotions have gotten your adrenaline pumping, you may have to do more than talk. Try running around the block, chopping wood, or cleaning the oven, and see if it doesn't help.

Feelings that aren't talked out or worked out, build up and are eventually acted out. For example, if you don't express your anger in words, it's likely you will throw something, blame others, or slam doors. It's a lot better than holding it in, but these actions can hurt others and things.

So, let your home be a safe place to talk out and work out the negative! And let the process begin with you.

"He who walks in his uprightness fears the Lord, but he who is perverse in his ways despises Him."
—Proverbs 14:2, NKJV

DR. KAY KUZMA

Getting Through the Tough Times

Every marriage goes through tough times. Like the couple celebrating their fiftieth wedding anniversary expressed, "We've been married forty-seven happy years and three bad ones." The important thing is to not give up. Just like the stock market goes up and down, so do marriages. If you stick in there, yours will likely rebound—if you're both committed to each other for life.

That doesn't mean you have to be a victim of abuse. To be respected, set healthy boundaries and stand up for yourself without putting your mate down. You can choose how you would like to live, rather than merely reacting to how your mate is treating you. You are valuable and deserve love, support, and healing.

Here's a thought to hold on to: "when troubles come your way, consider it an opportunity for great joy. For you know that when your faith is tested, your endurance has a chance to grow" (James 1:2, 3, NLT).

It may seem impossible to you now, but going through these difficulties can strengthen your character and make you a better person—and a more desirable mate.

"So let it [endurance] grow, for when your endurance is fully developed,
you will be perfect and complete, needing nothing." —James 1:4, NLT

Giving Love Is Good Math

Here's a thought that can change your marriage: "Love is the one treasure that multiplies by division. It is the one gift that grows bigger the more you take from it. It is the one business in which it pays to be an absolute spendthrift. You can give it away, throw it away, empty your pockets, shake the basket, turn the glass upside down, and tomorrow you will have more than ever."

I have no idea who wrote those words, but I'm convinced that giving love away with abandon can change your marriage—and your life.

Try this: Write down some ideas about how you could show your mate that he or she is loved supremely. Brainstorm. Read a good book on marriage and add to your list. Interview a friend for more ideas. Then when your mate is not expecting it, start throwing your love away in his direction. Be lavish. Pour it out in heaping doses, not wishing for anything in return, and see what it does for you.

I have a feeling as you divide up your love and give it away you'll find your personal pleasure multiplied.

"No one has ever seen God. But if we love each other, God lives in us, and his love is brought to full expression in us."
—1 John 4:12, NLT

DR. KAY KUZMA

Getting Your Man to Talk

Never "talk to" a husband. Instead, your goal should be to "talk with" him. How? By learning how to be a good listener.

That's right! If you've got a spouse who doesn't talk much, hone your listening skills. Stop what you are doing when he does talk, look him in the eye, lean forward, look interested, don't interrupt, but interject words of interest like, "Oh," "Interesting," "Great," or "Tell me more."

Then when you do respond, sweeten your words. Put a lilt and a little excitement in your voice. Don't flood him immediately with woeful tales of your trials and tribulations. Be positive! Nothing attracts a man like an upbeat, happy, optimistic woman! Let him find it in you—not another woman!

Husbands around the world would rise up and call their wives "blessed" if wives would sprinkle their conversations with a little more honey and a lot less grit!

"Kind words are like honey—sweet to the soul and healthy for the body." —Proverbs 16:24, NLT

Nobody's Perfect

The tyranny of the ought," is what psychologist Karen Horney calls perfectionism. It can rule your life and in the process make you and your mate miserable.

Yet, on the surface it seems good. Who could fault the wife who was trying to do her best, striving to reach goals, and choosing to be a peak performer. And wouldn't you be proud of the husband who is known for his dependability and attention to detail.

The problem is when perfectionism becomes more important than people. Being terribly correct becomes terribly wrong when it causes tension, fighting, and hard feelings between you.

If you have perfectionistic leanings, you're going to have to work on becoming a more flexible person. Lower your expectations to realistic levels. Don't take yourself so seriously. And don't complain about your mate's imperfections.

Put people first—especially your mate. When you do, it's hard to be a perfectionist, because nobody's perfect!

"I don't mean to say that I have already achieved these things or that I have already reached perfection. But I press on to possess that perfection for which Christ Jesus first possessed me." —Philippians 3:12, NLT

DR. KAY KUZMA

As You Think, You Become

Have you ever wondered how a stake and a chain could keep a five-ton elephant in place? It's only because the elephant learned as a baby that when he tried to get away, he couldn't. As an adult, it's not the stake that's holding him in place, it's his old pattern of thinking.

The same with a fish put in a glass tank with feeder fish swimming on the outside of the tank. In an attempt to eat, the fish hits against the glass until he ceases to even try, and will likely starve to death even with feeder fish in his tank.

Marriage partners sometimes act a lot like elephants or fish. The patterns of thinking they developed as children affect their adult behavior. Some won't even try to do certain things because they failed when they were children. Others excuse their inappropriate actions and refuse to change by saying, "That's how I've always done it!"

If this sounds a lot like you or your mate, it's never too late to begin developing healthy thinking patterns with positive phrases like, "I can." "It is better to try and fail, then never try at all." "Failure is the stepping-stone to success." Or "With God, all things are possible."

---

*"For as he thinks in his heart, so is he." —*Proverbs 23:7, NKJV

Magic Moments With Your Family

Ionce read a story about a father dancing with his pajama clad three-year-old son in his arms. I shut my eyes and I could imagine dad twirling and dipping, and his son holding tight, burying his head against dad's shoulder.

And then I remembered magic times like that with our children. Watching the night sky for falling stars. The animal rides to bed, when our little ones would climb on their daddy's back and proclaim the animal they wanted to carry them to bed. Away they would go bucking, swaying, or hopping down the hall.

I remember watching the big round harvest moon come up as we stood on the roof of our house to see it peek from its hiding place behind Mount San Gorgonio.

Those were magic moments of memory that will never fade. I hope you're busy creating those magic moments with your family. Remember, kids leave home, but memories never do!

"For where your treasure is, there your heart will be also." —Luke 12:34, NKJV

DR. KAY KUZMA

Miracle-Working Love

Have you ever yearned for some magic to turn your marriage around? Something to heal your aching heart, restore hope and confidence, spark creativity, motivate you to service, free you from tyranny, and transform the unloved into the beloved?

Who wouldn't welcome such a miracle? You might be willing to pay a high price for its formula. But you don't have to. It's available to everyone—free.

What is this miracle? Love. Yes, that's right; love! I didn't invent it. But I'm fortunate to have experienced it. And I've discovered that nothing else in the world has the life-changing power love has.

No one is too young or too old to not benefit from a little love, either as a recipient or as a giver. And the beauty of it all is that there's always an abundant, unending supply. For when you give love away, it has a way of coming back. *Love creates love.*

"And now abide faith, hope, love, these three; but the greatest of these is love." —1 Corinthians 13:13, NKJV

How to Live to Enjoy Your Grandchildren

You've probably heard all the facts about the importance of exercise! People who are physically active tend to weigh less, have lower blood pressure and serum cholesterol levels, and as a result, are at much lower risk for heart disease than their inactive counterparts.

But that's not all: Exercise relieves anxiety and stress and helps lift depression; it clears the mind by stimulating circulation; it improves sleep; it strengthen the bones by helping them retain calcium and other essential minerals—and all of these things slows the aging process.

But for too many couples, facts alone aren't enough to get them out of their slippers and into their walking shoes. You've got to make a decision and have the will to do it!

Let me make a suggestion: Exercise together. Find something that you both enjoy. Put on an aerobics DVD. Pump iron or do jumping jacks. Walk the dog together. Plan an early morning bike ride with another couple.

I want you to live to enjoy your grandchildren, so get up now—and get moving!

"May you live to enjoy your grandchildren!" —Psalm 128:6, NLT

DR. KAY KUZMA

What Happened to the Man You Married?

Remember that man you married? He was a pretty nice guy, wasn't he? He treated you special, gave you little gifts, and probably helped you with the dishes.

Have you ever wondered what happened to that wonderful guy? Women across the country complain that a married man's greatest fault is his lack of attention. But maybe it's not all his fault.

The problem is the hunt is over. Men have captured their game (you), so they are now off to other challenges like making it to the top of their career ladder, running a marathon, catching the fish that got away, or rebuilding their '58 Olds. Now what men need in a wife is a companion.

Don't expect your man to get involved in your life until you get involved in his. The challenge is to become a recreational companion to your husband. Show you're interested in his world, and he'll be a lot more interested in yours.

"And the Lord God said, 'It is not good that man should be alone; I will make him a helper comparable to him.'"
—Genesis 2:18, NKJV

Understanding Each Other

When Jan and I got married, I was ignorant of our different temperaments and how they might affect our relationship. I did know he was very methodical, organized, and wouldn't think of starting his day without a list. In my book, lists were to let people know what you wanted for Christmas!

After marriage we got along just fine as long as he didn't tell me what to do. But we started to tangle when we had children. He'd tell them what to do, and then, since he wasn't home, he would expect me to make sure they did it. If I didn't, I'd get blamed.

The crisis came when I said, "Enough. I'd rather live alone than be constantly blamed for something that wasn't my fault." He was shocked. He had no idea I didn't like having him organize my life and tell me what to do.

That was the beginning of us being more open with each other—and respecting our differences!

"Nevertheless let each one of you in particular so love his own wife as himself,
and let the wife see that she respects her husband." —Ephesians 5:33, NKJV

DR. KAY KUZMA

Polish Your "Self-Concept" Mirror

Your behavior is like a mirror that reflects to your mate how valuable he or she is. If you smile, he feels great about himself. If you frown, she feels rejected or inferior.

Jack brought his wife a flower he picked. Without emotion, she took it from him and dropped it in the trash. Her mirror reflected to him that he was worthless. Tess greeted her husband with a hug. Instead of responding, he said, "Let me put this stuff down," and then he ignored her, picked up the mail, and headed to the study. Her self-concept plummeted.

Ted came up behind his wife and whispered "I love you," in her ear. She felt adored. Her self-concept soared. Kaitlyn reached over and squeezed her husband's hand in church. He could see in her behavior that she enjoyed touching him—and he felt valuable.

Your self-concept mirror is always working—always reflecting.

What does your mate see reflected in you? Hopefully he sees a pretty wonderful guy. Hopefully she sees someone who is valuable and absolutely adored. If not, maybe your mirror needs a little polishing.

"But we all, with unveiled face, beholding as in a mirror the glory of the Lord, are being transformed into the same image from glory to glory, just as by the Spirit of the Lord." —2 Corinthians 3:18, NKJV

Are You Looking for Romance?

Are you looking for romance to brighten up a dull life? Romance! Just the thought of being swept off your feet in a love so intense that it takes your breath away, sounds wonderful. And every marriage needs the anticipation, surprise, excitement, and fun that romance brings to a relationship.

But, romance will never fill you with complete satisfaction, unless its foundation is the kind of love expressed in 1 Corinthians 13: Love that is patient, kind, and not envious, boastful, proud, rude, selfish, or easily angered. You want a love that keeps no record of wrongs and doesn't delight in evil but rejoices with the truth; one that always protects, trusts, hopes, perseveres, and never fails.

An impossible dream?

No, not when you truly respect each other and love unselfishly, placing your own happiness in the happiness of another.

"Greater love has no one than this, than to lay down one's life for his friends." —John 15:13, NKJV

DR. KAY KUZMA

Facing a Financial Fall

One of the major causes of stress in a marriage is money. It's especially tough when one is a spender and the other a saver. It's like two people in a canoe paddling in opposite directions. You might be able to handle things for a while, but if you're not careful you'll find yourself being swept over the falls of financial difficulties. Here's how to know if you're in trouble:

- If you don't really know how much you owe and are afraid to add it up.
- If you find yourself writing checks and postdating them.
- If you're afraid to let your spouse know how much you've spent.
- If you don't have an emergency fund to handle expenses for three months.
- If your credit balance grows each month.
- If you have no savings plan.

Are you heading toward a financial fall? If so, you've got to paddle together toward shore, establish a budget, and faithfully live by it! Control your money—don't let it control your marriage.

"For what is a man profited, if he shall gain the whole world, and lose his own soul?" (Or lose his own marriage?)
—Matthew 16:26, KJV

Get Rid of the Garbage

Can you imagine never taking out the garbage? Instead, you start piling it in one room; and when that room fills up you start filling another.

Yuck! What a ridiculous thought. Garbage is something you throw out, not something to keep.

I once saw a cartoon with these words, "Every night before you go to bed leave your worries on the curb, 'cause that's where they pick up the garbage."

I thought about that. Your negative emotions—your worries—are a lot like garbage. If you keep them around, they'll smell up your life and pollute your marriage. And just like no one wants to be around a pile of garbage, if you're absorbed with worry, no one—not even your spouse—will want to be around you!

Instead, put your worries out on the curb—give them to the Lord—and fill your life with something positive. Then notice how much more your mate will enjoy your presence.

"Finally, brethren, whatever things are true, whatever things are noble, whatever things are just,
whatever things are pure, whatever things are lovely, whatever things are of good report,
if there is any virtue and if there is anything praiseworthy—meditate on these things."
—Philippians 4:8, NKJV

DR. KAY KUZMA

Spice Up Your Life With Dreams

When your house is a mess and the kids are crying and your spouse is working late at a demanding job—or has a headache, do you ever feel like escaping from it all?

Running away doesn't solve problems. You may blot the frustrations of family out of your mind for a few hours, but they will hit you head-on every time you return.

Instead, consider your priorities carefully. Your spouse and your relationship should come first. Is the job really that demanding, or is he or she trying to escape too? What fun things have you done together recently?

Spice up your marriage with a romantic weekend for the two of you where you have time to make some plans for your future. Without a dream, the messy house, crying kids, and lack of husband support or a headachy wife, spell frustration and boredom! A dream helps you look at life with anticipation instead of dread.

Things just aren't as depressing when you have something fun to look forward to. Make some plans today.

"Those who plan what is good find love and faithfulness." —Proverbs 14:22, NIV

Damaging "Don't Care" Habits

Just because you're married, it doesn't mean you should let down your hair and forget your manners. To keep your marriage strong, avoid these damaging habits that say you don't care.

1. *Forgetting.* You shouldn't have to depend on your spouse to remind you of important events. Get a calendar or make sticky note reminders. If you're techy—program your computer to remind you. Keep a family calendar in a prominent place and consult it daily. Be proactive!

2. *Skipping hellos and goodbyes.* How you greet your spouse or say goodbye is like a marriage barometer. It reveals the climate between the two of you. Make your homecomings memorable. Say goodbye with passion. If your mate is busy, take a minute to find him or her. Just don't disappear.

3. *Telling secrets to outsiders.* What you say and do in your marriage, should stay there. Don't triangle a family member or friend into your conflicts. Don't tell your friends something that might embarrass your mate. You must be able to trust your mate with your innermost secrets and know that's where they'll stay.

"In You, O Lord, I put my trust; let me never be ashamed." —Psalm 31:1, NKJV

DR. KAY KUZMA

Don't Let Stress Batter Your Marriage

Are you tired, upset, jumpy, irritable, depressed, angry, or bossy? If so, it just might be that you've caught the most contagious disease in the world, and if you don't do something about it immediately, it will attack your spouse— and eventually the whole family.

No, I'm not talking about AIDS. But it's a killer just the same. It's STRESS.

You might not have thought of stress as being contagious, but here's how quickly it spreads: A wife comes home stressed out from her job and criticizes her husband for not helping more around the house; the husband yells at the kids for not helping their mother; the children retreat to their rooms and begin fighting over their toys. Within fifteen minutes, the whole family is behaving irrationally.

The answer is to master stress—don't let it master you and your marriage. Whatever it is that's causing chronic stress, make a change, *even if it's just a change in attitude*. Beat stress before it beats you.

"Oh, love the LORD, all you His saints! For the LORD preserves the faithful." —Psalm 31:23, NKJV

Words Can Destroy More Than Your Marriage

Regardless of how dysfunctional a mate might be, or what he or she might have done in the past, it's important that you always frame any comments about the other in the best possible light. This is especially true when the kids are listening. Your kids can't change the fact of who their parents are—and who they are will affect their own self-concepts. Put your spouse down, and you are not only destroying your marriage, but your children as well.

As children get older and ask questions about their parents' lives, they have a right to know facts including those that are negative. But these facts should be given without moralizing and, if possible, something favorable should be shared at the same time. For example, "Yes, it's true your mother was addicted to alcohol and therefore it was difficult for her to adequately meet your needs, but she was a fun-loving person and she loved you supremely."

If you're dealing with a dysfunctional mate and your marriage is suffering, get professional help so changes can be made without destroying your kids. Don't let hidden agendas and unresolved bitterness cause you to say things that may wound your mate—or your kids—for life.

"The faithful love of the Lord never ends! His mercies never cease." —Lamentations 3:22, NLT

DR. KAY KUZMA

What Do You Want From Your Marriage?

It's easy to get so wrapped up in the daily routines of life that marriage partners may forget that the ultimate goal is not a clean house or a spotless wardrobe, but a vibrant marriage relationship.

What would turn your marriage into a vibrant one? Be specific. What about at least thirty minutes of meaningful talk time each day? Time alone to enjoy each other without cell phone or computer interruptions; a happy attitude when you're with each other; a weekly date; celebrating special days; getting abundant compliments; patience and kindness expressed to each other; or discussing tough issues without selfishness getting in the way.

If you want your mate to be honest, cooperative, responsible, and have a positive self-concept and a sense of humor, look at yourself. Are you modeling those characteristics? You're in this marriage together. Don't expect more of your mate than of yourself.

"For he who lacks these things [faith, virtue, knowledge, self-control, perseverance, godliness, brotherly kindness, and love] is shortsighted, even to blindness." —2 Peter 1:9, NKJV

Marriages Need Venting Time

When people want to make important points at board meetings, they plan strategies so their ideas will be most receptive. Timing is crucial. Yet in marriage, couples often drop emotional bombs with little thought as to their mate's ability to handle the content at that particular moment. Ill-timed explosions destroy relationships.

You've been stewing all day. You can hardly wait until your husband gets home to let him have it. As he walks in the door, you explode, "Why can't you . . . and if you ever do that again . . . Why are you persecuting me?" He had a lovely evening planned for the two of you, but your ill-timed outburst destroyed it.

To prevent a surprise attack, every marriage needs a planned venting time when both are rested, well fed, emotionally stable, and have time, without interruption, to deal with what might be a lengthy discussion.

Just the act of putting an item on the venting-time agenda will likely prevent the impulsive explosions that are so destructive to marriages.

"Who is wise and understanding among you? Let him show by good conduct that his works are done in the meekness of wisdom." —James 3:13, NKJV

DR. KAY KUZMA

Humor That Hurts

The joke may be funny to you, but it could be like a punch in the pit of your mate's stomach. Humor can hurt. Don't joke about personal things like your mate's freckles, acne, hairstyle, or growing waistline. Emphasize the positive. Don't highlight things your partner would rather have hidden.

Don't joke about mistakes the other has made. Mistakes are embarrassing enough. Don't add insult to injury by jesting and making fun of the other. Laugh with your spouse, not at him or her.

Don't tell jokes about your mate's family or friends—and don't tease your partner about things you know are sensitive subjects. You might get by with telling something once, but repeating the same embarrassing story again and again rubs salt into the wound.

So to be safe, keep your jokes on neutral subjects, like sports, TV, fashion, or politics, so you and your mate—and your friends can safely laugh together.

"Woe to you who laugh now, for you shall mourn and weep." —Luke 6:25, NKJV

Don'ts for Decision-Making

Do you sometimes feel overwhelmed with all you have to do? Here are a few don't for decision-making that may help you to get control of your life:

- Don't say Yes to others when you'd rather say No.
- Don't make an immediate decision about taking on another responsibility. Instead say, "I always think about decisions overnight. Call me back tomorrow." Then check with your mate and the Lord before saying Yes.
- Don't assume other people's agendas or emergencies are yours. You don't have to be the solution to other people's problems.
- Don't do too many things at once. Multitasking can be counterproductive. Focus on doing fewer things, but doing them well.
- Don't accept impossible deadlines. Give yourself some "pad" time.

And then, when it comes to something your mate wants to do, say Yes instead of No, and you'll find life a lot more meaningful!

"'Everything is permissible for me'—but not everything is beneficial." —1 Corinthians 6:12, NIV

DR. KAY KUZMA

Keys to Good Communication

Does your mate walk away when you're trying to talk? Do you both seem to go for days without saying much more to each other than "Hi" and "Goodbye," or "Please pass the potatoes"? Do you wonder what your mate is thinking, but when you ask, get "nothing" for an answer. If so, you need some pointers to help you communicate more effectively. Here are ten:

1. Take time to listen. Stop what you're doing and look in the other's eyes.
2. Show an interest in your mate and what he or she says.
3. Don't tell your mate what to do; ask politely.
4. Don't interrupt. Wait until he or she is finished or when your opinion is asked for.
5. Let your body language say you are really interested in what your mate is saying.
6. Be a responsive listener. Instead of trying to make your own point, respond to what is being said.
7. Take what your mate says seriously and show an interest in his values, goals, and ideas.
8. Share your positive and negative feelings and encourage your mate to do the same.
9. Notice your mate's body language and factor it into what is being said.
10. Avoid lecturing, criticizing, and analyzing.

"Therefore whoever hears these sayings of Mine, and does them, I will liken him to a wise man who built his house on the rocks" —Matthew 7:24, NKJV

Words Versus Word Pictures

You've heard it said that a picture is worth a thousand words. I could advise husbands and wives to quit the quarreling and not be so abstinent, antagonistic, touchy, combative, belligerent, and contentious. Or from the wisest man who ever lived, I could give you some word pictures that get the message across much more clearly.

Solomon says in Proverbs 27:15, "A quarrelsome wife is as annoying as constant dripping on a rainy day" (NLT). In fact, it's better to live in the corner of an attic or in the desert than in a lovely home with a quarrelsome, complaining spouse (Proverbs 21:9 and 19, NLT).

Here's another word picture: "A quarrelsome person starts fights as easily as hot embers light charcoal or fire lights wood" (Proverbs 26:21, NLT). Or if you meddle in a quarrel that doesn't concern you, it's "like one who takes a dog by the ears" (Proverbs 26:17, NKJV).

Finally, picture yourself as a broken-down city without walls. That's what you're like if you don't practice self-control (Proverbs 25:28, NKJV).

I hope you get the picture and stop the quarreling before you lose your temper, get hurt, destroy your marriage, and find yourself living alone!

"Incline your ear and hear the words of the wise, and apply your heart to my knowledge." —Proverbs 22:17, NKJV

DR. KAY KUZMA

Put-Downs or Lift-Ups

Amarriage license is a license to love, honor, and be willing to meet the needs of the other. It's not a ticket to hurt another person. Yet husbands and wives so often say and do things that put their partners down, rather than lift them up.

For most people, "put-downs" have more force than "lift-ups." In fact, if I'd give a numerical value to them, I'd say it's about ten to one. In other words, it might take ten, or more, kind words and actions to even begin to overcome the damage of one put-down.

Many husbands and wives have no idea of the barbs their thoughtless words carry. Because marriage is a binding relationship, many think they can let all their ugly emotions hang out, without considering the feelings of the people they live with. How much better to respect each other, walk in love, and be kind! That's what a marriage license is all about.

"And walk in love, as Christ also has loved us and given Himself for us, an offering and a sacrifice to God for a sweet-smelling aroma." —Ephesians 5:2, NKJV

Keep Your Pilot Light On

Passion is like a gas stove. It heats up more quickly when you want it if you keep the pilot light burning. If you want to have a hot time in bed at night, you've got to learn to keep your pilot light burning throughout the day with kind words, gentle actions, thoughtful deeds, little gifts, contagious laughter, playful looks, focused attention, generous forgiveness, and teasing touches.

Marriages that get better the longer they last aren't built on great sex alone. Instead great sex is built on meaningful marriages that are filled with loving interactions throughout the day.

If some day you discover your pilot light has gone out—if you get busy and forget to call, rush to work without that goodbye kiss, or leave a mess for your spouse to pick up—don't expect instant sex at bedtime. If you do, sex is downgraded to duty rather than love, and you are cheating yourself and your mate out of the ultimate joy that God-designed sex brings to a marriage. Good sex takes time. Keep the pilot light burning twenty-four hours a day!

"He brought me to the banqueting house, and his banner over me was love. Sustain me with cakes of raisins, refresh me with apples, for I am lovesick." —Song of Solomon 2:4, 5, NKJV

DR. KAY KUZMA

Don't Be the Prosecutor

Questions can be great conversation starters, "How did things go today?" Questions can be a great way to get information, "What did the doctor say?" But the interesting thing about questions is that they can encourage your mate to talk—or shut up!

The problem is that too many questions make people feel they're on the witness stand being cross-examined by the prosecuting attorney. "Why didn't you tell them your plan? When do you think you'll know? What did you say? Where did you park the car? How will they know?"

Too many questions and you'll put your spouse on the defensive. The result? He or she feels criticized and condemned and too often walks away in silence or frustration.

Since asking questions is not always the best way to get information, try giving your mate these openings, "You look like you've really had a great time." "I remember how upset I was when that happened to me." Or, "I'd love to hear about the meeting."

"Congenial conversation—what a pleasure! The right word at the right time—beautiful!"
—Proverbs 15:23, *The Message*

Communicating Feelings

When husbands and wives choose to communicate their feelings, it's much easier to meet each other's emotional needs.

For example, one busy morning Pat got up early, folded the wash neatly, and put it in the ironing basket. A few minutes later her husband, looking for his shirt, pawed through the wash and left it in a jumble. Pat was angry and realized that if she didn't say something, she would remain angry all day and would not be able to concentrate on her work. So she said, "Bill, I'm angry at the way you left the clothes in the ironing basket."

"Sorry, sweetheart," he replied as he came into the room. "I'll refold them."

Pat couldn't believe her ears! What if she had *criticized,* "Bill, why can't you do things right"? Or *threatened,* "You better fold them again—or else"? Or *demeaned* him, "What's wrong with you?" Or given him a *guilt* trip, "All you do is mess things up"? Well, you can guess the answer. He would have probably slammed the door and headed off to work.

But because she had chosen to communicate her feelings, her husband was able to respond in such a way that she no longer had any reason to be angry.

"Listen, please, and let me speak; You said, 'I will question you, and you shall answer Me.'" —Job 42:4, NKJV

DR. KAY KUZMA

Be a Cheerful Receiver

Imagine you go to a lot of effort to find an extra special gift for your mate. With great anticipation you wait as it is unwrapped. Then instead of saying thanks and joyfully accepting the gift, your spouse says, "Why did you get me this? I'll never use it. We don't have the money. You'll just have to take it back. I'd never be caught dead in something like this!"

How would that reaction make you feel? You'd probably think, *See, if I ever get you something again!*

Your attitude about receiving can have a major effect on your spouse's attitude about giving. Be excited about what is given to you, and you'll likely get other gifts. Whatever the gift, show a genuine attitude of appreciation—and an element of joyful surprise. This is what makes giving fun. And in this world so often filled with the spirit of selfishness, it's important that husbands and wives have a good time giving to each other!

"So let each one give as he purposes in his heart, not grudgingly or of necessity; for God loves a cheerful giver."
—2 Corinthians 9:7, NKJV

Painful Love

The idea that pain is a part of love, or that you're not worthy of love without pain, can have a devastating effect on a person's life and can destroy a marriage.

One young woman said the only time her parents told her she was loved was after abusive spankings and painful punishment. Now she says, "I'm afraid to love anyone, because I'm afraid I will hurt them just as I was hurt. I mistrust kindness and reject any show of affection because I'm afraid of the pain that I learned was associated with these feelings. I'm afraid to reach out to anyone, to give them a spontaneous hug, or to become emotionally intimate. I always have to keep my distance, so neither one of us will end up hurting the other. Touch, instead of being something pleasant, is something that makes me tense."

Can you see how growing up with the script that the only way to get love is to endure pain can destroy a marriage? If you or your mate has difficulty with any of the above behaviors, get help. Forgive your folks or the person who hurt you. Then begin enjoying pain-free love—both the giving and the getting—which is a must for a meaningful marriage.

"Let us get up early to the vineyards; let us see if the vine has budded, whether the grape blossoms are open, and the pomegranates are in bloom. There I will give you my love." —Song of Solomon 7:12, NKJV

DR. KAY KUZMA

Chip Talk

Too many spouses have verbal diarrhea. From the moment they walk in the door, their mouths just keep running. Regardless of how much they know on a subject, they have a comment to make.

People married to mates with chronic verbal diarrhea often quit trying to compete. They just shut up and let the other person go on talking.

If your spouse has quit talking to you, it could be that you've been talking too much. Here's what I suggest:

Have you ever tried to eat just one potato chip? Impossible, isn't it? You've got to have more. You want to create this same desire in a spouse. Don't throw your mate the whole bag of chips at once. Serve one chip at a time. Say "Sweetheart, you'll never believe what happened," and then stop. Let him ask for more. Another chip, "It was truly incredible." Stop. Stir up his interest until he's ready to listen. The secret to good communication is not to drown your mate with too much or starve him with too little.

"Those who control their tongue will have a long life, opening your mouth can ruin everything." —Proverbs 13:3, NLT

Taking the Spiritual Temperature of Your Lives

Are you and your spouse on fire for the Lord? Or are you among the frozen chosen?

With world events moving so rapidly toward the completion of the great controversy between Christ and Satan, it's time to stand up like Joshua and declare, *"But as for me and my house, we will serve the LORD"* (Joshua 24:15, NKJV).

If you were to stand up today, what would you say about the spiritual temperature of your marriage? How would you evaluate the condition of your spiritual life as a couple?

Sometimes an illustration can help you see things more clearly. Try this: each of you draw a thermometer and then mark on the thermometer how "hot" you think each of you are for the Lord. Sit down before looking at each other's drawing, because the results may be more truthful than you want. For example, your mate may rate your spiritual temperatures lower than you think. Then talk about how you as a couple can turn the temperature up!

"I don't mean to say that I have already achieved these things or that I have already reached perfection. But I press on to possess that perfection for which Christ Jesus first possessed me." —Philippians 3:12, NLT

DR. KAY KUZMA

Character Improvement Increases the Passion

Women enjoy looking up to their men, and when they do it's easier to love them. But looking up doesn't mean a husband has to have money, position, and recognition. In fact, these things have very little to do with a good marriage.

It is character that is most important. Every woman wants to know she is married to a good man. One who is kind, cooperative, and honest.

If she catches him cheating on the income tax, overhears him telling off a neighbor, or finds he has a weakness for pornography, that is what kills desire.

You may have made some mistakes in the past. Your wife will respect you if you own up to them, rather than blame others! Don't give up on yourself. You can change if you really want to.

Character is built by the little decisions you make. Why not start today to purify your own character, and see if it doesn't increase the passion in your marriage?

"Kiss me and kiss me again, for your love is sweeter than wine. How fragrant your cologne; your name is like its spreading fragrance. No wonder all the young women love you!" —Song of Solomon 1:2, 3, NLT

Taking Responsibility for Your Mistakes

Have you ever tried to squirm out of an uncomfortable spot by blaming others? It happened at the beginning of time. When Adam ate the forbidden fruit, he blamed Eve. And Eve? She blamed the serpent. And six thousand years later, we're still doing it! Just picture yourself in these common situations:

Company comes. You're behind schedule; things are in a mess. You turn to your husband: "If you had helped, this wouldn't have happened."

You receive a speeding ticket. Angrily, you turn to your wife. "Why didn't you get ready quicker? I wouldn't have had to drive so fast."

It takes guts to own up to your mistakes, but your mate will respect you if you do. So the next time you goof, honestly say, "It's my fault. I'm sorry." You'll feel better about yourself when you take personal responsibility for what you do and your mate will love you for it.

"And the LORD God said to the woman, 'What is this you have done?' And the woman said, 'The serpent deceived me, and I ate.'" —Genesis 3:13, NKJV

DR. KAY KUZMA

Getting Along With the In-Laws

If you have in-law problems, you're not alone. According to one survey, in-law relationships were the number one problem of 25 percent of the couples seeking marital counseling, and was the number two problem of another 60 percent.

Blessed is your marriage if you get along with your in-laws. But if you don't, here's what you can do.

1. *Live your own life.* Don't borrow money from them or in any other way become dependent on them for your existence. If you use them, there is a greater chance you'll feel controlled by them, whether they mean to be controlling or not.

2. *Listen*, but don't let what they say make you feel inadequate or guilty. Don't let them control your feelings. You can choose to respond to them in love.

3. *Leave.* Believe it or not, moving across the country, especially for the first few years, is a great way to loosen the tie from parents who can't understand that you've cut the apron strings.

"For this reason a man shall leave his father and mother and be joined to his wife, and the two shall become one flesh."
—Matthew 19:5, NKJV

Custom-Made Romance

What does romance mean to you? To one, it might mean a candlelight dinner. To another, a backpacking trip where you sleep under the stars. A husband might enjoy seeing his wife in a pretty negligee. One wife said, "All I want is for my husband to come to bed clean-shaven!" Another said, "Romance is having my husband arrange for someone to clean the house and then surprise me with Chinese take-out." Or as another couple said, "It's ending up together in a bathtub filled with scented bubbles—and making sure our kids don't come home early from their evening activities."

Most enjoy being swept off their feet with thoughtful surprises—but some don't like surprises. For others, romance isn't so much a moment as it is a thoughtful way of life.

If you don't know what romance means to your mate, your romantic plans can backfire. For example, the cruise a husband plans only to discover his wife gets seasick, the flowers he got for her birthday that she's allergic to, or the surprise reservations at a fancy restaurant that takes time away from preparing for an early morning business presentation.

Here's what I do know about romance: The more you can customize it to fit your mate's likes and interests, the more it will mean.

"In the morning sow your seed, and in the evening do not withhold your hand; for you do not know which will prosper, either this or that, or whether both alike will be good." —Ecclesiastes 11:6, NKJV

DR. KAY KUZMA

Solving Child-Rearing Differences

Disagreeing over how to raise a child can be a thorn in an otherwise rosy marriage, unless you follow these ten commandments:

1. Resolve your differences as soon as they arise.
2. Promise to not disagree in front of the children.
3. Attend a parenting class together and discuss new methods of child rearing.
4. Read parenting books together.
5. Don't blindly follow your parents' methods.
6. Own up when you make mistakes with your children.
7. Bite your tongue when tempted to say, "I told you so."
8. Promise each other that if either wants to go for family counseling, the other will agree to go also.
9. Establish ground rules for open communication.
10. Pray that God will give you an understanding heart and insight into how to "train up a child in the way he should go."

"Direct your children onto the right path, and when they are older, they will not leave it." —Proverbs 22:6, NLT

Reach the Heart Before the Mind

It is a well-known fact that children are more cooperative if they know that their teachers really care about them. They don't have to misbehave to gain attention, feel important, or make their point. Carter Bayton, a teacher in an inner-city New York school, expressed it this way, "You have to touch the heart before you can reach the mind."

The same principle holds for marriage partners. Too many times a husband or wife tries to force an idea or opinion onto his or her mate using logic and reason, only to be met by stubborn resistance. The natural impulse is to force the issue. But the more couples argue the point, the more closed-minded each becomes.

Force never works. The old axiom is true: "A person persuaded against his will is of the same opinion still." So the next time you want to influence your mate, don't hit him or her over the head with it. Instead try reaching the heart with kindness, thoughtfulness, gentleness, patience—and all those other heart-softening, loving actions, and you might just be surprised what a difference it will make.

"I will praise the LORD, who counsels me; even at night my heart instructs me." —Psalm 16:7, NIV

DR. KAY KUZMA

Try an Italian Kiss!

I'll never forget that evening when my husband, Jan, walked through the back door and called, "Kids, come quickly, I'm going to give your mother an Italian kiss!" Guess who came quickly? I wondered what he had in mind.

With the children watching, Jan took me in his arms, bent me over backwards and gave me a wonderful, romantic kiss.

The children then said, "We want one too." And they each got their own version of an "Italian kiss."

That incident has become one of our family's favorite memories. It was a fifteen-point encounter.

I'd give Jan one point for thinking enough about me on his way home to plan such an unusual and romantic greeting. I'd add a couple of points for just being together. Then three more points for talking, four for looking at each other, and five for touching. Add it up and it comes to fifteen points. And that's a meaningful—and memorable—experience.

Why don't you surprise your mate with an Italian kiss tonight?

"The voice of my beloved! Behold, he comes leaping upon the mountains, skipping upon the hills."
—Song of Solomon 2:8, NKJV

The Twenty-Four-Hour Wait Policy

If you're tired of being in debt, you need to establish the twenty-four-hour wait policy, and put an end to impulse buying.

When you or your spouse find something you want, don't argue about whether you should buy it. Instead write it on your want list. Make it a policy that you will only buy things that are on your want list for at least twenty-four hours—and only if you have the money or a good plan to earn the money. This policy avoids most conflicts over finances.

To determine the item's value, calculate how many working hours it would take to earn enough money to purchase it. Ask, "Is it worth it?" If you still want it after twenty-four hours, make a plan and start saving. Then circle the date when you will likely have the money.

Impulse buying is a habit that dooms families to a lifetime of debt and often makes marriages miserable. The twenty-four-hour wait policy may be just what your marriage needs.

"Take heed and beware of covetousness, for one's life does not consist in the abundance of the things he possesses."
—Luke 12:15, NKJV

DR. KAY KUZMA

Don't Worry—Be Happy

What is the most important personality trait to have in a spouse? There are many, like loyalty, respect, and thoughtfulness. But the one that tops my list is happiness. That's right! I don't want a miserable mate, because misery loves company—and is contagious. And I don't want to be miserable!

Nor do I want to take on the responsibility of trying to make my husband happy. I don't want to hear: "If you would just get a better job, then I'd be happy. If you would just be home more, then . . ."

Happiness is a choice. If you let your attitude toward life be dependent on circumstances, then you're doomed for a life of misery, ill health, fatigue, negative relationships, and failure—because bad things happen.

If you're not a naturally happy person, then for your mate's sake, begin focusing on the positive things in your life. When tempted to worry, stop yourself and fill your head with positive self-talk. "Today is not that bad." Then smile, sing, or whistle a happy tune.

"So don't worry about tomorrow, for tomorrow will bring its own worries. Today's trouble is enough for today."
—Matthew 6:34, NLT

Antidote for Loneliness

Just because you're married, doesn't mean there won't be times when you might be lonely—and it's not just when your mate isn't home. Feelings of loneliness can hit when you're sitting next to each other and your partner is too involved in something else to pay any attention to you.

Some people are more social than others. Your mate may be a loner and needs more quiet time alone than you do. That doesn't make it wrong. You just need to accept these differences, rather than resent them—and find another relationship to meet your needs. (And I'm not talking about the man or woman next door!)

If you're lonely, make Jesus your constant Companion. Your dynamic relationship with Him will cushion loneliness, heartache, rejection, and all the other negative emotions that you might suffer. Get to know Jesus better. Claim His promises. Every minute you invest in developing your relationship with Christ is time well spent—and the very best antidote there is against loneliness in marriage.

"Delight yourself also in the Lord, and He shall give you the desires of your heart." —Psalm 37:4, NKJV

DR. KAY KUZMA

Don't Let Your Past Ruin Your Present

If you're not careful, the hangovers from a past divorce can destroy your present marriage. The best advice is preventive: Before jumping into a new relationship, get divorce counseling and clean up your past. Healing takes time.

But chances are, it's too late for that advice! And even if you did everything "right," the past, like a bad nightmare, can occasionally come back to haunt you. When that happens, here are three things you must remember:

1. *You can't be married to two people at the same time!* Your loyalty is to your new spouse. You must put his or her welfare and feelings first. If the two of you can't solve this problem together, or your spouse expresses irrational jealousy, get marriage counseling NOW.
2. *Full disclosure is essential.* You may have gotten married thinking your past would just fade away, so it wasn't important to share everything. If problems surface, don't blame others or skirt the truth. Now is the time, within reason, to tell all.
3. *Eat humble pie!* Don't try to blame others. Admit failure and ask forgiveness.

"And be kind to one another, tenderhearted, forgiving one another, just as God in Christ also forgave you."
—Ephesians 4:32, NKJV

Matrimony or Purgatory

A bishop was administering confirmation to a group of young people and asked a nervous child, "How does the catechism define matrimony?"

The child hesitated for a moment and then said, "It is a state of terrible torment which those who are compelled to undergo for a time to fit them for a better world."

"No, no," interrupted the parish priest. "You've mixed up the definition of *matrimony* with the definition of *purgatory*!"

"Let it be." The bishop smiled. "How do two priests like you and me know that the child is not right?"

Wait a minute. That parish priest better not be right! Instead, I'd suggest a great marriage is more like being marinated. In other words, two people become so blended in commitment and purpose that instead of two distinct flavors—there is only one!

Unless this is your goal, you can expect that your marriage relationship will, at times, be a lot more like purgatory than matrimony!

"'For this reason a man shall leave his father and mother and be joined to his wife, and the two shall become one flesh'; so then they are no longer two, but one flesh." —Mark 10:7, 8, NKJV

DR. KAY KUZMA

The Chain of Command in Marriage

If a man was to be the head, as Paul seems to be saying in Ephesians 5:22 and 23, then shouldn't it follow that he is the first in command, the top dog, number one, the head honcho, the final word, the king of his domain, the CEO of the family, and definitely in charge of his wife, who is to be submissive to him?

Careful! Don't take these words out of context—and don't try to interpret them without understanding the cultural treatment of women in the first century. When Paul wrote Ephesians, wives had NO rights—they were the possessions of their husbands, who were in total control and could get rid of them by simply putting their things outside the door.

So what Paul was really doing was elevating the wife's position. Instead of ruling their wives, men were to treat them as Christ treated the church—which He died for! Scripture says that although Christ was equal with God, He emptied Himself and took the form of a servant (Philippians 2:7). Christ also declared that to rule was to serve and to be over was to be under (Mark 10:42–45; Luke 22:24–27; John 13:13–16).

Interesting, isn't it?

"Wives, submit to your own husbands, as to the Lord. For the husband is head of the wife, as also Christ is head of the church; and He is the Savior of the body." —Ephesians 5:22, 23, NKJV

The Symbolism of Touch

Have you ever wondered why most wives enjoy having their husbands appropriately touch them in public? It's not only the security of holding hands or the warmth of being embraced, but it's symbolic as well. It says to the world, "This is my man; we belong together; I am special to him." A thoughtful, loving touch symbolizes acceptance to both husbands and wives—and to those observing.

When two people hold hands, others know they are a couple and not just random acquaintances going in the same direction. An even closer relationship is symbolized when a husband puts his arm around his wife. An arm around the shoulders usually means a more casual relationship, while an arm around the waist symbolizes a more intimate one.

When the kids see Mom and Dad smooching in the kitchen or giving each other foot rubs they know their folks love each other.

Touch is symbolic of a meaningful relationship. Think about it. What does it say to others—including your kids—if they never see you as a couple touch each other?

"When I found the one I love. I held him and would not let him go." —Song of Solomon 3:4, NKJV

DR. KAY KUZMA

Psychological Attachment Versus Intimacy

Did you know it's possible to get married and have physical intimacy without psychological intimacy? That's right. A couple can have good sex: they can experience the pleasures of physical stimulation, the sensations of arousal and climax, and the bonding that results, yet miss the added pleasure of experiencing the oneness of psychological intimacy.

How is this possible? Psychological attachment and psychological intimacy are not the same thing.

Psychological bonding or attachment is brought about with touch. The more a couple physically stimulates each other, the more they feel attached. It's like the suction cups on an octopus's tentacles. The more touch, the more dependent they become on each other, regardless of personalities, interests, or cultural differences.

Psychological intimacy may include physical intimacy but is the result of a growing friendship—not sex alone—and it turns into the kind of love that will last a lifetime. The oneness that is God's ideal for marriage.

"I in them, and You in Me; that they may be made perfect in one, and that the world may know
that You have sent Me, and have loved them as You have loved Me." —John 17:23, NKJV

Getting to Really "Know" Each Other

If you played *The Newlywed Game* and were asked questions about your spouse, how would you do? Would you know what he would do with a million dollars? What is her dream vacation? His favorite book? Who was her most influential teacher? What is his or her attitude toward money? Success? Children? Employment? Different races? Street people? God? What expectations do you have for each other and your marriage? If there was one thing your spouse would like to change about you, what would it be? If you made three sacrifices for your mate, what would he or she want them to be? What makes your spouse feel most loved?

Just how well do you really "know" each other?

You may think that after all the time you've been married that you know about everything you could possible know, but the person he or she was when you married is not the same person you're married to now. Every day people change. If you let a few days go by without sharing the meaningful things in your life with each other, it doesn't take long before you're living with a stranger.

Why not take some time right now to get to know each other just a little better?

"So teach us to number our days, that we may gain a heart of wisdom." —Psalm 90:12, NKJV

DR. KAY KUZMA

Do Your Temperaments Tangle?

Chances are great that you married someone with a different temperament. Opposites attract—but they aren't the glue that holds a marriage together. That's why the best thing couples can do is accept each other unconditionally and work on changing themselves. For example:

If you're *sanguine* and enjoy having fun and being the center of attention, you may need to put others first and take time to really listen, rather than doing all the talking.

If you're *phlegmatic,* and avoid conflict, are easygoing, and dislike change, you may need to learn to talk through difficult situations rather than retreat and share your feelings rather than bottling them up.

If you're *melancholy,* you're probably a deep thinker with a perfectionistic bent. Learn to enjoy each day and try to be a little more spontaneous and cultivate friendships.

If you're *choleric,* you like to get things done and aren't afraid to tell others what they should be doing. You may need to relax and take more time to participate in fun activities.

Don't let your temperaments tangle up your marriage. You can choose to change.

"And whatever you do in word or deed, do all in the name of the Lord Jesus, giving thanks to God the Father through Him." —Colossians 3:17, NKJV

Before Children

Once you have children, your life will never again be the same. You will change—and so will your spouse. This isn't bad, it's just reality. That's why it's good to do everything you've ever wanted to do B.C. (that's Before Children). Then when the kids come along, you'll be ready and eager to move on into this awesome new chapter in your marriage.

So if you're in your early years of your life together and still have a choice, talk about what you would like to do before you have a baby—and begin making plans. Maybe it's taking that surfing trip to Costa Rica, motorcycling across the country, finishing your degree, or getting established in your dream job. Whatever it is, it will certainly be easier now than trying to work it in when you have to worry about meeting your baby's needs—as well as your own.

Above all, don't neglect your marriage. Children do best when they are born into a family where their parents adore each other and are totally committed to making their marriage last a lifetime.

"To everything there is a season, a time for every purpose under heaven." —Ecclesiastes 3:1, NKJV

DR. KAY KUZMA

What Do You Do With a Lazy Man?

I used to write a question and answer column for a weekly Christian journal where readers were encouraged to send me questions. I received the usual questions about disobedient children or teenage moral issues, but what surprised me was what was asked about marriage. Believe it or not, the number one issue that wives wrote me about was basically, what do you do with a lazy man.

One letter in particular said, "My husband has been looking for a job for twenty-two years. I have supported the family, paid medical bills, sent the kids to Christian school, while he's been basically lying on the couch. He doesn't even help around the house. I've had it? What should I do?" I think she was really asking, "Is it OK to divorce him?"

I think men need to know that one of the major things a wife needs from a husband is financial support. He doesn't have to earn much and most wives don't mind helping with the finances, *but he has to do something*! Marriage shouldn't be a free ride for a man—or a woman!

"The fool folds his hands and consumes his own flesh." —Ecclesiastes 4:5, NKJV

Love Is Patient

Why is patience the very first characteristic that the apostle Paul mentions when he defines love in 1 Corinthians 13? I've given it some thought and I'm convinced that it's a lot easier to be kind or not rude, envious, proud, or boastful—especially toward the family—than patient. But no characteristic is more important for a good marriage.

If you always interact with your mate with patience, here's what you will or won't do:

- You won't get upset when things go wrong or your spouse makes a mistake.
- You won't get angry easily or throw a temper tantrum.
- You will be understanding and give your spouse the benefit of the doubt.
- You will show mercy instead of justice.
- You will be gentle and forgiving rather than opinionated and forceful.
- You won't overreact, yell, or say hurtful things.
- You will take time to listen carefully.
- You will control your emotions and act rationally.
- You won't retaliate or fight back.
- You will take time to solve problems.
- You will hold on in tough times rather than bailing out.

If husbands and wives really practiced patience, just think what a difference it would make!

"Be completely humble and gentle; be patient, bearing with one another in love." —Ephesians 4:2, NIV

DR. KAY KUZMA

Marriage Is a Marathon

I watched the runners in the Kauai Marathon run by our house the other day, and I thought how much marriage is like a marathon. When you're running a 26.2 mile race, you don't decide one day and run the next. It takes a lot of planning and practice. I met one of the runners. He said he has been running marathons for four years, and keeps in shape by running ten or more miles a day, five days a week.

A marital engagement is like running the hundred yard dash. You sprint in order to win the prize, giving it everything you've got for a short period of time. Contrast this with a marathon. Few run to win. Most run to finish the race—hopefully in better time than the last.

It takes practice, plus endurance, to go the distance. You don't quit just because the weather isn't perfect, your shoelace breaks, or you get so tired you think you're going to die.

And that's the way it should be with marriage. You never know what you're going to encounter next, but regardless, you're committed to finish the race, and celebrate, knowing you gave it your best.

"Do you not know that those who run in a race all run, but one receives the prize?
Run in such a way that you may obtain it." —1 Corinthians 9:24, NKJV

Being First in Marriage

There is no room for selfishness in marriage. Two selfish people will not only destroy each other but also their marriage. Yet more husbands and wives need to determine to be first. Does this sound selfish or conceited? Well, it depends on what you want to be first in. Here's what I suggest: Determine that you will be first in . . .

- Saying I'm sorry.
- Greeting your mate.
- Smiling.
- Serving the other.
- Forgiving.
- Sharing.
- Writing a love note.
- Meeting the other's needs.

Too many marriages fail because both mates are waiting for the other to step up to the plate and do the honorable thing. "I will, if he will." "She needs to apologize first, then I'll forgive." "If it's that important to him, let him go first."

And what if neither is willing to go first? The marriage fails by default. In order to get a broken relationship back on track, it takes two proactive people who are both willing to go first.

"See then that you walk circumspectly, not as fools but as wise, redeeming the time." —Ephesians 5:15, 16, NKJV

DR. KAY KUZMA

Celebrity Marriage Models

For better and for worse . . . until death do us part." You probably recognize these words as part of the traditional marriage vows taken by couples looking forward to a life together filled with loving embraces, shared family activities, fun vacations, and good sex.

But what if marriage doesn't exactly turn out as expected? What if something terrible happens to one, and the fantasy marriage turns out to be twenty-four-hour care of a quadriplegic who can't even breathe on his own? Or maybe it's a progressive crippling disease that attacks one, threatens a promising career, and forces the couple to re-prioritize their dreams and goals for the future?

Standing in their tux and gown, holding hands, and repeating their wedding vows, a bride and groom never consider that the "worse" could happen to them. But if it does, there are some celebrity couples that have proved to be great role models of loyalty and commitment. You know who I'm talking about: Christopher Reeve and his faithful, encouraging wife, Dana, and Michael J. Fox and his beautiful supporting marriage partner, Tracy Pollan, have become models for the world of what marriage really means.

"A faithful man will abound with blessings." —Proverbs 28:20, NKJV

Avoiding Infidelity

Sex is God's special gift to each married couple. He ordained it at Creation when He made a man's and woman's bodies perfectly fit to physically come together as one. He even designed a little pizzazz into that coming together so that a couple would look forward to experience the delightful sensation again and again. Every time a couple makes love, it's like a symbol reminding them that they are committed to a one-flesh relationship forever.

To make sure couples don't misuse this gift, God established some rules about lust and adultery so these sins wouldn't destroy marriages. Jesus even went so far as to say a lustful eye was adulterous! As my friend, Alberta Mazat, once said, "This must have shocked the Pharisees!"

But if Jesus were walking this earth today, I wonder what He would say about off-color jokes, pornography, X-rated movies and DVDs, and the use of His incredible gift of a one-flesh relationship for manipulative, selfish, or even abusive purposes?

"But I say to you that whoever looks at a woman to lust for her has already committed adultery with her in his heart."
—Matthew 5:28, NKJV

DR. KAY KUZMA

I Love You Because . . .

How do I love thee? Let me count the ways" are the first lines of one of the most famous love poems ever written. Elizabeth Barrett Browning goes on to enumerate how she loves. For example:

"I love thee to the depth and breadth and height my soul can reach."

"I love thee to the level of everyday's most quiet need."

"I love thee freely, . . . purely, . . . with the passion . . ."

Her words are filled with an ethereal sound and rhythm that gives one a heightened sense of *agape* love. It would be well if every married couple, on a romantic moonlight night or sitting before a warm winter's fire, would read each other the entire sonnet.

But what if Browning had changed the first word of her poem from "How" to "Why?" Do you realize what a difference it would have meant? "Why do I love you?" implies that there are reasons you love your mate. What if those reasons cease to exist? What if beauty, talent, or skills are destroyed? Every mate wants to be loved just because he or she exists and not for some reason.

In marriage, show you appreciate good traits, but love as God loves—unconditionally.

"And I am convinced that nothing can ever separate us from God's love. Neither death nor life, neither angels nor demons, neither our fears for today nor our worries about tomorrow—not even the powers of hell can separate us from God's love." —Romans 8:38, NLT

Pocketbook Peace

Here's an interesting statistic: Men become more productive after marriage. They earn between 10 and 40 percent more than single men with similar education levels and job histories. Married couples pool their resources and save more. Plus, married couples receive more money from family members than singles.

If all these statistics are true, shouldn't married couples have more money? Why is it that financial conflict is the basis of so many divorces? My guess is that financial problems in marriage have less to do with the amount of money earned and more to do with problems of management.

If you would like "pocketbook peace" in your marriage, I'd suggest you start managing your money using Dave Ramsey's Financial Peace University principles. His "baby steps" include establishing a thousand dollar emergency fund, paying off debts, saving enough to cover three to six months of expenses, investing 15 percent of your household income, starting a college fund for the kids, paying off your home early, giving an honest tithe, and blessing others with your excess.

"For the love of money is a root of all kinds of evil" —1 Timothy 6:10, NKJV

DR. KAY KUZMA

143

When Your Mate Should Be Number Two

In order to have a healthy family, it's important to put your spouse first, before your kids or anyone else. There is one exception: When a child is being abused, your moral responsibility must be to protect your child.

Nina had an explosive personality. It was the only role model she knew. Matt loved her in spite of her temper, but then came the children.

It hurt Matt to see the kids being severely criticized, blamed for things they didn't do, and harshly spanked. At first he didn't interfere. Slowly it came to him that they were being abused. He got professional advice. When he finally said, "Either get help and learn how to discipline without abuse, or I'll have to move out and take the kids. I will not let you destroy them."

That shocked Nina. At first she didn't take Matt seriously. Two weeks later, she came home to an empty house. The end of the story is that she got help and their reunited family was stronger than ever.

Sometimes a mate has to be number two in order to realize how important it is to change dysfunctional behavior.

"Whoever causes one of these little ones who believe in Me to sin, it would be better for him if a millstone were hung around his neck, and he were drowned in the depth of the sea." —Matthew 18:6, NKJV

Making Yourself Clear

Have you ever thought you made your point clear, only to realize your spouse didn't get the message? This can be a real problem between husbands and wives.

Women are known to be more indirect in their speech while men are more focused. A wife may say something like, "Honey, let's go to bed early tonight," and then is surprised when she announces around nine o'clock that she's going to bed and he doesn't follow.

"But you never said you wanted me to come to bed early," he says.

"Well, you should have known that's what I meant."

"Then why didn't you just say you wanted me to come to bed with you at nine?"

If you don't want to be blamed for not catching the message when your mate throws you a curve, ask for clarification. "Did I hear you correctly? You said . . ." and put the statement into your own words. On the other hand, don't presume you've made yourself clear if your spouse doesn't respond. Ask, "Sweetheart, did you understand what I'd like? I'm not sure I made myself clear."

"Let every man be swift to hear, slow to speak, slow to wrath." —James 1:19, NKJV

DR. KAY KUZMA

Anything You Can Do . . .

Too many married couples are in competition with each other. They are like Annie Oakley and Frank Butler singing the song Irving Berlin wrote for the 1946 Broadway musical *Annie Get Your Gun:* "Anything you can do I can do better; I can do anything better than you!"

Competition will kill a marriage. Janelle was a popular and talented musician. She married a man who also played the piano. He constantly criticized her playing, which forced her to practice even harder. When she continued to excel, he began demeaning her in other areas. Their marriage, obviously, didn't last very long.

When you marry, you become one—physically and emotionally. When one hurts, you both feel the pain; when one fails, you both feel the disappointment; and when one wins, you both celebrate. You help, support, and encourage your mate to be the best he or she can be because when you do, you're actually helping yourself.

The only competition that's good for marriage is when both are trying to outdo each other in showing unconditional love and utmost respect.

"Let nothing be done through selfish ambition or conceit, but in lowliness of mind let each esteem others better than himself." —Philippians 2:3, NKJV

You Can Fill Your Own Love Cup

When you realize your love cup is low, its contents being displaced by negative emotions, remember, you have the power to refill your cup with something positive.

First, *admit you are low*. There is nothing wrong with being low. Staying there is the problem. That's when you become depressed and begin to deal with others in unloving ways.

Second, *don't expect your spouse to fill you up*. It's nice when it happens, but you can't control others.

Third, *not every problem needs to be handled immediately*. In fact, most problems are handled more effectively after you gain control. If you feel ready to explode with words and actions that will empty someone else, you will feel depressed and guilty if you act out your feelings.

Instead, exercise. Shout your feelings to the wind or tell God. Then find a love-filling Bible text to meditate on. Next, do something nice for yourself. And for an overflowing cup, do something nice for your mate!

"You prepare a table before me in the presence of my enemies; You anoint my head with oil; my cup runs over."
—Psalm 23:5, NKJV

DR. KAY KUZMA

Rules for Conflict Resolution

No two people think alike, have the same interests, and make the same choices. Over the years couples usually grow closer—but they still won't always agree. So, how do couples successfully solve conflicts? Here are ten rules they live by:

1. No conflict is more important than our marriage.
2. Never go to bed angry.
3. Be truthful and play fair.
4. Don't fight in front of the kids or others.
5. Treat each other with respect: No put-downs, hurtful criticism, or bringing up the past.
6. Stick to the facts instead of personal opinions and feelings.
7. No physical violence or harsh angry touching.
8. Call "time-out" if tempers begin to flare.
9. Every problem has a solution.
10. Never mention divorce.

"Do all that you can to live in peace with everyone." —Romans 12:18, NLT

When Life Begins

Three mothers were discussing when life begins. The first said, "Life begins at conception. Do you realize that at just eighteen days an embryo has a detectable heartbeat!"

The second listened but offered a different opinion. "No," she said. "Life really begins at birth. When you can cuddle your newborn, look into your baby's eyes, and nurse her."

The third mother shook her head. "Life begins," she said, "when the kids leave home—and the dog dies!"

Well, I don't know what stage of life your marriage is in, whether you're thinking about having children, actually expecting one, rearing a dozen and dreaming about your emancipation day, or enjoying your grandchildren. But whatever stage it is, I hope you're living each day to the fullest, because when you get to the golden years and the kids have left home, you want to make sure your marriage is strong and vibrant enough to carry you through the retirement years. I want you to be able to honestly say, "Life begins again for us each day and our marriage just keeps getting better and better!"

"Rejoice in the Lord always. Again I will say, rejoice!" —Philippians 4:4, NKJV

DR. KAY KUZMA

Keep a Why-Not List

Most people love surprises—as long as they aren't embarrassed by them. I loved it when my husband would burst through the back door and call, "I've got this great idea." Usually it was some exotic vacation plan or something fun to do with the family, like watching the fireworks by sitting on the roof of our house.

Don't let your marriage get bogged down in boring routine. Instead, occasionally break out of your rut and say, "Why not!"

The problem for me was that I wasn't very creative and it was easier to do the same old thing again and again than come up with something new. That's why I think married couples need to keep a "Why-Not" list of crazy things they could do, and then when the time is right, announce, "Why not?"

Here are some things that we put on our list: Why not ride our bikes through the neighborhood park on a full-moon night? Why not double date with our good friends for Valentine's Day? Why not celebrate New Year's Day by jumping into the icy-cold swimming pool?

Isn't it time to say *why not,* and make a memory for your family?

"It is useless for you to work so hard from early morning until late at night, anxiously working for food to eat; for God gives rest to his loved ones." —Psalm 127:2, NLT

Peace or Problem

It's Kyle's job to do the laundry. He does it—but in his own way. Early in the morning he starts the first load. Then it's off to work. When he comes home, he puts the first load into the dryer and starts the second. When the first is dried, he stuffs it into the basket and then puts the second load into the dryer. Often bedtime comes before the second load is dry. The next morning he dumps both loads on the sofa where he can watch TV as he folds. If he runs out of time, the clothes sit there all day until he gets home from work.

When Carla sees the laundry on the sofa she goes into orbit. She has tried to change him, but it hasn't worked. Should she confront him again? It depends on what she wants—peace or a potential problem?

After all, Kyle is doing the laundry. If she confronts him, he could get defensive, tell her she can do the laundry if she wants, or get angry. Is it worth it? Carla decided she would just move the laundry, or if she had time, fold it herself.

Next time you find yourself in a similar situation, maybe it's time to choose peace.

"I am for peace; but when I speak, they are for war." —Psalm 120:7, NKJV

DR. KAY KUZMA

Two Are Better Than One

Remember the Bible text about it is good when two are together, so when one falls down the other can help him up? That's what marriage is all about.

Actually falling into a ditch doesn't happen often in marriage, but psychologically falling is another story. Being hit with bad news, criticism, and unjust treatment can easily cause a person to fall into the ditch of disappointment, depression, despair, sadness, and frustration.

When this happens to one, it is vitally important for the other to listen and empathize. The objective, however, must be to pull the other out of the ditch of negative feelings without falling in yourself. Here are some techniques you may want to try.

- Make a list of all the good things about the bad news. Talk positive.
- Exercise and eat good, nutritious food. Feeling good physically helps you feel better psychologically.
- Do something that keeps your mind on other things. Read a good book to each other, finish a project together, visit friends, or do something to help others who are in a worse situation! Time is usually a good healer. Give it time to work!

"Two are better off than one, because together they can work more effectively. If one of them falls down, the other can help him up. But if someone is alone and falls, it's just too bad, because there is no one to help him."
—Ecclesiastes 4:9, 10, TEV

Shortcut to a Good Marriage

The best way to spell love is T-I-M-E. This is true for raising children—and for maintaining a good marriage. When does a husband or a wife feel most loved? When his or her mate gives focused attention.

Yet the home, the place couples spend most of their time, is usually filled with built-in distractions: the mail needs to be opened, bills paid, the furniture dusted, the dirty clothes washed, the weeds need to be pulled, the grass mowed, and the kids taken care of. The list of things to do seems endless. Couples can't just ignore all these things, but things can get in the way of a good marriage.

That's why couples—especially those with children—should take a second honeymoon every year. In addition, they should invest in a weekly date night and no less than thirty minutes of focused attention time each day. There is no shortcut. It takes time to really show each other focused attention. It takes T-I-M-E to maintain a good marriage.

"There's a right time for every thing, every deed—and there's no getting around it." —Ecclesiastes 3:17, *The Message*

DR. KAY KUZMA

Couples' Communication and Divorce

There are three marriage communication styles:

The *Validators* calmly air their views, try to understand the other's position, and reach a compromise.

The *Volatile,* although deeply romantic, these couples jump at the chance to launch a into rip-roaring argument and try steamrolling their way to victory.

The *Conflict-Avoidant* may argue, but sidestep issues, or agree to disagree and drop the subject.

Here's a shocking statistic: It's not the number of arguments a couple has that drives them to divorce, it's the ratio of positive things versus negative things that are said or done. If the ratio is five to one, *couples with the same communication styles* aren't likely to divorce. The problem is where there is a mismatch, probably because a mismatch leads to more negative things said!

What should couples learn from this study by Robert Levenson and John Gottman? They should recognize their communication styles and respect each other, rather than allowing this difference to increase their conflicts. And regardless, they should give each other far more positive messages than negative.

"Here is a simple, rule-of-thumb guide for behavior: Ask yourself what you want people to do for you, then grab the initiative and do it for them." —Matthew 7:12, The Message

---

Self-Therapy for the Blues

Clinical depression can kill a marriage. It is an illness that needs professional help and medication. But most people who say they are depressed are just having a down day. When this happens, *for the sake of your marriage,* take control of your life. Here's a self-therapy program:

Make a list of everything you need to do. Then prioritize it, and tackle the first item. Celebrate when each task is finished. As you see yourself making progress in accomplishing the things that need to be done, you will feel better about yourself and your situation.

Next, begin a physical therapy program. Exercise the muscles of your head and face. Give yourself a good head rub, and then smile. Exercise the rest of your body by walking briskly in the fresh air for at least fifteen minutes three times a day!

Finally, get rid of any bitterness you have toward anyone. Forgive him or her and wish for him or her the very thing that you like most in your own life. In other words, begin living by the Golden Rule, "Treat others as you would have them treat you."

"You will show me the path of life; in Your presence is fullness of joy; at Your right hand are pleasures forevermore."
—Psalm 16:11, NKJV

DR. KAY KUZMA

Listening to Feelings

A frustrated wife wrote, "My husband is always telling me what to do, when all I want him to do is listen and try to understand me!"

I answered, "He may be uncomfortable with the expression of feelings. When something is wrong, the immediate tendency for most men is to fix it. But you can't hold on to feelings and fix them as you would a flat tire on the car. You've got to get your feelings out so you can deal with them. Yet your husband probably doesn't realize this, and therefore he tries to fix your feelings by telling you what to do."

It takes practice to be a good listener. I suggest you start when you have no major emotional issues facing the two of you. Look in each other's eyes and let each talk for two minutes without interruption, with the other occasionally saying, "Oh," "Yes," "That's interesting," or some other expression that says, "I'm listening." Then give the other a turn. Practice makes perfect!

"And walk in love, as Christ also has loved us and given Himself for us." —Ephesians 5:2, NKJV

Keep Your Love Bank Account Full

A marriage must not be viewed as the end of the hunt, but the beginning of an adventure of finding fresh and creative ways to say "I love you."

Willard Harley's love bank concept can help you evaluate how well you are doing. The idea is that each individual has a love bank in which each significant person in his or her life has an account. If an encounter is positive, a deposit is made to that person's account. If negative, a withdrawal.

During the honeymoon, couples have little difficulty making significant deposits in each other's love banks. But afterward, unless the earlier attentions are continued, the negative encounters subtract from the balance and a marriage can grow stale and boring. If at the same time someone else's account grows, a marriage is ripe for an affair.

Just how full is your account in your mate's love bank? Why not make a significant deposit right now by romancing your mate with a fresh and creative way of saying "I love you"?

---

*"And walk in love, as Christ also has loved us and given Himself for us, an offering and
a sacrifice to God for a sweet-smelling aroma."* —Ephesians 5:2, NKJV

DR. KAY KUZMA

Open Your Home to Others

My friend told me about a stranger whose visit ran over into family time, which was an important part of their family's day. She began to look forward to his departure, not even listening to what he had to say. She was almost ready to tell him that he would need to leave because they had other plans, when she found herself wondering if he were lonely.

"Suddenly," she said, "this visitor was no longer an inconvenience." Instead, it became an opportunity to share a little warmth and friendship that always radiates from a happy family, and they cheerfully invited the stranger to join their evening activities.

This couple didn't have much of the world's riches to give away. They were struggling to make ends meet. But what they had, they gave. And a number of hours later, a much happier man left than the one who had come. As they waved goodbye, they realized just how blessed they were to have each other and thanked the Lord.

What does your family have to share? Is a little time for the lonely too much to ask of you?

"When God's people are in need, be ready to help them. Always be eager to practice hospitality."
—Romans 12:13, NLT

Why Are Men and Women SO Different?

Every cell in a man's body is different from a woman's because of chromosome patterns established at conception. But there's more: At seven weeks, the male brain is bombarded with nearly ten times more testosterone, while on the eighth week, the female's brain is hit with great amounts of estrogen-progesterone. Then sixteen weeks after conception, the male brain is doused with a biochemical bath that severs most of the left-to-right brain transmission wires, or *corpus callosum*. This makes it more difficult for males to cross brain hemispheres when thinking. Instead they tend to solve problems primarily with the left side of their brains, which is more logical and analytical, while women more easily use both hemispheres when thinking.

The result is a man's brain is like a laser beam that is able to focus on a goal or persevere toward winning. The disadvantage is that he may tune out relationships. A woman's brain tends to react more like radar—aware of everything around her—especially relationships.

No wonder God said it wasn't good for man to be alone. Couples need each other to complement their own way of thinking and make them more complete. Celebrate your differences. Don't let them be a source of conflict!

"And the LORD God said, 'It is not good that man should be alone; I will make him a helper comparable to him.'"
—Genesis 2:18, NKJV

DR. KAY KUZMA

A Godly Model for Marriage

The best way to understand the concept that two individuals in marriage can become one, is to study the Trinity. The Godhead is Three Entities, Each with different roles but One in purpose, love, and leadership.

The Father's Role: Jesus says, "The Father loves the Son, and shows Him all things" (John 5:20, NKJV).

The Son's Role: "My Father is greater than I" (John 14:28, NKJV). "The Son can do nothing of Himself, but what He sees the Father do. . . .I do not seek My own will but the will of the Father who sent Me" (John 5:19, 30, NKJV).

The Holy Spirit's Role: In John 14:26, Jesus says that the Holy Spirit is sent by God to "teach you all things, and bring to your remembrance all things that I said to you" (NKJV).

Theologian Beatrice Neall writes, "The Trinity is characterized by mutuality. Leadership is fluid, passing from one to the other, and the three members make joint decisions and derive fulfillment from carrying them out. Each affirms and glorifies the others. The secret of this unity is love." Replace the word "Trinity" with "Marriage" and you have a great model for a great marriage.

"Finally, all of you should be in agreement, understanding each other, loving each other as family, being kind and humble." —1 Peter 3:8, NCV

Money or Marriage?

Newlyweds Sarah and Drake had a combined monthly income of over four thousand dollars; but it didn't buy them happiness, and their marriage was suffering. They became convinced that going back to school would be a positive move for them. But how could they when they couldn't earn that kind of money if both were in school? Frustrated with the thought of having to give up their dreams, they went for counseling.

"What do you really want?" the counselor asked. "Money or marriage?" Then he challenged them to live for a year on a fourth of what they were making and put a couple hundred dollars a month in an emergency savings fund.

It seemed impossible—and it would have been if they had stubbornly held on to their current lifestyle. Instead, they chose to humble themselves and control their money instead of allowing money to control them. The result was, they put their marriage back together ;and four years later, they were living their dream. As the counselor Willard Harley puts it, "Happy is the couple who tries to live on what they need, not what they want."

"Better is a little with the fear of the LORD, than great treasure with trouble." —Proverbs 15:16, NKJV

DR. KAY KUZMA

Lessons From Your Parents' Marriage

What have you learned from your parents' marriage that you either want to incorporate into yours, or avoid? It's a great husband-wife discussion question—especially early in marriage.

Regardless of how dysfunctional your family of origin may have been, there are some things you learned that have helped you become a better person. Hopefully, you have modeled the good, and have chosen not to repeat the bad.

What did I learn from my folks? I learned how important touch was. I loved it when Dad came up behind Mom in the kitchen and gave her a lingering hug or patted her bottom. Those spontaneous expressions of affection let me know my folks really loved each other. It made me feel secure, and I wanted that in my marriage. And what did I learn from the things I didn't like? I vowed I'd go to bed at the same time as my spouse—even if he was an early bird and I was a night owl.

I think I've been a better spouse from learning from my folks' marriage. I think you'll be too.

"Honor your father and your mother, that your days may be long upon the land which the Lord your God is giving you." —Exodus 20:12, NKJV

Ten Rules for Avoiding Intimacy

Communication is the key to intimacy. So, if you *don't* want intimacy, do the following!

1. *Act as if nothing ever bothers you.* Don't share your feelings—especially not the negative ones.
2. *In a conflict, retreat.* Pout. Give your mate the silent treatment. Then get even.
3. *Always keep busy.* Make sure your spouse knows productivity is more important than your relationship.
4. *Look out for number one.* Make sure you're first. Fight to win.
5. *Schedule your time and stick to it.* Limit lovemaking, conversation, or play to specific times.
6. *Always stand up for yourself.* Don't back down or be made to feel weak by compromising.
7. *When something goes wrong, blame others.* Make them feel guilty and responsible for your dissatisfactions, failures, or unhappiness.
8. *When you find something you don't like in your spouse, try to change it.*
9. *Don't tell your spouse what you want and need.* Tell yourself, If my mate really loved me, he or she would know.
10. *Insist on doing things the way your parents did.*

And if you do decide to follow these rules, get yourself a good divorce attorney!

"The lips of the righteous know what is acceptable, but the mouth of the wicked what is perverse."
—Proverbs 10:32, NKJV

DR. KAY KUZMA

Ten Rules for Being a Good Communicator

Good communicators are good listeners. In addition, they . . .

1. *Maintain a safe climate to say whatever is on their minds without being afraid of being demeaned.*
2. *Practice self-disclosure.* Be willing to confront and share thoughts about unresolved issues.
3. *Discuss touchy subjects.* No topics should be off-limits for discussion.
4. *Presume the best about the other.* No character assassinations—and don't jump to conclusions.
5. *Count to ten before responding.* Let James 1:19 be your guide. "Everyone should be quick to listen, slow to speak, and slow to become angry" (NLT).
6. *Discuss one issue at a time.* Stay on the topic. Don't dump everything on your spouse at once.
7. *Keep it private.* Don't share your disagreements with family or friends. Get counseling if necessary.
8. *If wrong, swallow your pride and admit it.*
9. *Make Psalm 19:14 your daily prayer.* "May the words of my mouth and the meditation of my heart be pleasing to you, O LORD, my rock and my redeemer" (NLT).
10. *Ask God to be your Mediator.* Pray, pray, pray.

When you follow these rules, you'll find yourselves celebrating your amazing feeling of oneness. It's important that you do, for behavior that's rewarded, is repeated!

"How sweet are Your words to my taste, sweeter than honey to my mouth!" —Psalm 119:103, NKJV

Marriage Traditions

Traditions! Tray and Jen go four-wheeling in the Colorado Rockies every October to enjoy the autumn colors. Each anniversary, Liem and Sarah return to their honeymoon cottage. Luke and Denise get tickets to the Laker's first home game of the season.

Some couples hold hands when they pray, or kiss afterward. Others have weekly date nights, or celebrate the day they were married, such as the twentieth day of each month. Some have a movie night, Sunday sleep-in with breakfast in bed, or pizza Thursdays.

Holidays are a great time to establish marriage traditions for your family, like cutting your own Christmas tree, caroling on your neighbor's porch, or making popcorn balls and fudge.

Jan and I have a tradition that we celebrate every Friday night. After supper we read an inspirational story and then take turns recalling what we were most thankful for that week.

Traditions are great memory-makers. They help define the uniqueness of your marriage. They are something to look forward to—and something that helps you recall the good things in the past. Traditions enrich marriages. I just wish we had started a few more!

"And Joshua said to all the people, 'Behold, this stone shall be a witness to us, for it has heard all the words of the LORD which He spoke to us. It shall therefore be a witness to you, lest you deny your God.'" —Joshua 24:27, NKJV

DR. KAY KUZMA

Be the Recreational Companion of His Dreams

Here's typical premarriage behavior: She sees him jog by her house. He's good looking and always alone. She buys a pair of jogging shoes and sits on the porch as he jogs by. He notices. They begin to jog together each morning. She goes fishing with him. They watch the Super Bowl together. He knows he has found the girl he wants to marry.

After the honeymoon, he says, "Sweetheart, get your shoes on and let's go jogging." She replies, "Jogging? I hate jogging!" And his dream of having a recreational companion for life is shattered.

Did you know that finding a girl who will be his recreational companion is at the top of most men's lists of what they want in a wife? The problem is, she gets busy, finds other activities she enjoys, and he goes off with the guys to watch a tennis match or play golf.

Wives, if you don't want to be a golf "widow," forget the housework, get someone to watch the kids, and start enjoying the recreational activities that your husband loves. If you're fun to be with, you are his number one choice. But if you say "No" too often, he just might find someone else.

"A good wife is her husband's pride and joy; but a wife who brings shame on her husband is like a cancer in his bones."
—Proverbs 12:4, TEV

What Is Your Love Language?

Have you ever tried to talk with someone who spoke a different language? It's frustrating, isn't it?
Well, you may not know it, but you and your mate might be trying to say "I love you," to each other in different languages, and the message just isn't getting across. Author Gary Chapman suggests that there are five love languages. Which one is your primary language? How about your mate?

- Words of encouragement
- Acts of service
- Gifts
- Spending time together
- Touch and physical closeness

Here's an interesting fact: Not only do people feel loved in a certain way, but they will tend to give love in the same way.

If your love language is gifts and you give a gift, your mate is likely to say, "Thanks, but I just wish we could spend more time together, or you'd hold my hand, or you'd be more encouraging, or you'd do something to help."

Check with your mate. It just might be you've been trying to love each other in two different languages!

"Can two walk together, unless they are agreed." —Amos 3:3, NKJV

DR. KAY KUZMA

Don't Step on Each Other

Good marriages require good *physical boundaries* about who can touch you and under what circumstances; good *mental boundaries* so you can have your own thoughts and opinions; and good *emotional boundaries* to help each of you take ownership of your own emotions.

Specifically, *without* boundaries . . .

- A spouse can feel used by the other taking advantage of his or her willingness to carry more than his or her share of home responsibilities.
- One mate ends up taking responsibility for the other's emotions—trying to make one happy or placating one if angry. Or one can blame, withdraw, or ridicule, hurting the other in an attempt to feel better himself or herself.
- One spouse almost always ends up controlling the other. Too often, one becomes the aggressor, using anger, withdrawal, or manipulation to get his or her way.
- One can easily be violated when a mate becomes involved in an affair.
- Unhealthy habits can become destructive compulsions like workaholism, sexual addictions, or alcohol, and other drugs. And the other spouse, rather than saying No, becomes co-dependent by either taking abuse or enabling the habit to continue by trying to protect the other's reputation.

"Finally, my brethren, be strong in the Lord and in the power of His might." —Ephesians 6:10, NKJV

Meeting Each Other's Needs

When Janie's emotions are in a tangle and her husband, Cooper, takes time to lovingly listen and empathize with her, something interesting happens. She feels drawn to meet his sexual needs. That's the way God designed the psyche of a woman.

On the other hand, after Sean spends time with his wife, Kris, listening to the things that happened to her during the day and meeting her emotional needs, he feels drawn to the bedroom. He doesn't really expect a sexual payoff, but more often than not, their hugs and kisses lead to love-making. That's the way God designed the psyche of a man.

The good thing is that's how God designed that married couples should relate to each other.

The bad thing is what if a man takes time to meet the emotional needs of another woman? Her natural impulse is to meet his sexual needs, while he unconsciously thinks he deserves it. And an affair can result.

The good thing is affairs rarely develop when the basic needs of a husband and wife are being met within a marriage.

"He makes the whole body fit together perfectly. As each part does its own special work, it helps the other parts grow, so that the whole body is healthy and growing and full of love." —Ephesians 4:16, NLT

DR. KAY KUZMA

Don't Crush the Flower

Allan was determined to change Jill's outgoing, impulsive, vibrant personality into a more stable, responsible one like his. He tore her down, told her what to do, and threated her if she didn't shape up. He even decided that her job should be to keep the checking account balanced because he thought it would be good training for what he considered her "out-of-control" personality.

One day his pastor said, "Allan, don't crush the flower in Jill." Allan was so busy trying to change Jill that he hadn't noticed that her spontaneous, happy nature was disappearing.

When Allan began to love his wife for the person she was, instead of trying to change her into someone like himself, the bubbly personality that he had fallen in love with returned. In the process Jill began to respect Allan and determined to work on becoming more responsible.

It is said that if your husband or wife is a different person after marriage than the one you married, it may be your fault. In trying to make him or her over, you destroy the very person you fell in love with! Don't let this happen to you.

---

*"This is how we know what love is: Jesus Christ laid down his life for us. And we ought to lay down our lives for our brothers and sisters." —*1 John 3:16, NIV

Get Out and Get Help

Both husband and wives can be guilty of abuse. But within marriage, men are more frequently the physical abusers. Mona didn't realize she was being abused; she thought it was a married woman's role to put up with male dominance. Suzie thought she deserved it. She reasoned that if she were just a better wife, it would stop. But it didn't!

It is estimated that half of all women at some time in their lives will be battered by a man who also "loves" them. And it occurs among all races, religions, ethnic groups, and educational levels. The sad fact is, according to the Centers for Disease Control, a woman is in nine times more danger of a violent attack in her own home than on the streets.

Wives, here's a word of warning: If your husband has an anger issue and you or your children are being battered, verbally or physically, get out—or you'll get hit again! Help is available. Don't be conned into thinking you've got to stay because you have no money, no place to go, and "what would the neighbor's think—or the church members?"

Sometimes the only thing that will convince a man to get the help he needs to overcome his abusive behavior is the loss of his wife—and possibly jail time! It's sad, but it's true.

"And let none deal treacherously with the wife of his youth." —Malachi 2:15, NKJV

DR. KAY KUZMA

Avoiding an Affair

Your marriage relationship started out by just thinking about the other person. Then you spent time together. Next you talked and talked and talked. That's how your friendship grew and the connection strengthened. Then came long, loving looks and meaningful touches. That's the process that every couple goes through to become bonded and finally decide to marry and make a lifelong one-flesh commitment to each other.

Just because you're married doesn't mean you won't be attracted to other people and have opposite-sex friendships. But if you don't understand the dangers of what I call the "lingerings," then you're ripe for an affair. Maybe not a physical one, because you know adultery is a sin, but an emotional one, where you grow closer to another person than your mate.

What are the "lingerings"? That's when you linger in your *thinking* about another person. And you linger *spending time* with them. Finally, you linger *talking, looking,* and *touching*—and before you know it you are emotionally bonded!

If you don't want that to happen to you—keep the "lingerings" for your mate!

"So teach us to number our days, that we may gain a heart of wisdom." —Psalm 90:12, NKJV

Women and Words

Did you know that each day women have twice as many words that they need to say than men? Some estimate the number may be as high as thirty thousand.

So here's what happens: When hubby comes home, he's running on empty. He has already exhausted his supply of words at work. He greets his wife, having no idea that she has another 27,382 words that she needs to use up before bedtime. All he wants is a little quiet time. All she wants is a lot of talk time.

Because her need to communicate is the greatest, she should take the responsibility for initiating a conversation and for keeping it going. The last thing she should do is to say something that might trigger the silent treatment. Nor should she drown him with a flood of words.

Instead, she needs to learn to say just enough to pique his interest and motivate him to consider her perspective. And since the first three minutes of a conversation set the tone for the entire discussion, she needs to make sure they're noncontroversial. The last thing she wants is for him to walk out and leave her alone with all those unsaid words.

"A word fitly spoken is like apples of gold in pictures of silver." —Proverbs 25:11, KJV

DR. KAY KUZMA

Living the Forgiveness Lifestyle

It was a small thing: "Sweetheart, where is the old VCR player?"

"Sorry, honey. We hadn't used it in years, so I gave it to the church for their yard sale."

"You mean, you gave it away? What about my old movies?"

"I gave them away too. I was just trying to get rid of the clutter."

"How could you? I loved those movies."

Are you catching the gist of the "conversation"? How would you finish it?

It depends on the lifestyle you're living. If you merely do what comes naturally, you'll "end" the silly argument with someone getting hurt. Tempers skyrocket, slams and accusations are thrown that hurt feelings! Simply put, the natural lifestyle is to out-think, out-talk, and outwit your partner until someone's in the outhouse!

The forgiveness lifestyle is completely different. Couples living with the spirit of forgiveness in their hearts, don't allow anger and resentment to build. They desire reconciliation, not punishment. They are quick to forgive and reconcile. And chances are they'd end the conversation with a reaffirmation of love: "Honey I love you, that's much more important than some old VCR machine!"

"Go ahead and be angry. You do well to be angry—but don't use your anger as fuel for revenge. And don't stay angry. Don't go to bed angry. Don't give the Devil that kind of foothold in your life." —Ephesians 4:26, 27, *The Message*

The "Perfect" Mate

Did you marry the wrong person? Of course you did—if you were looking for the perfect mate. Everybody does, because there is no such thing.

The problem is your faulty perception of marriage. If you think marriage means finding a partner who caters to your every whim, perfectly complements your personality, meets your many needs, makes you happy, and provides everything you want in life, forget it.

Instead, to have a meaningful marriage, unselfishly attempt to be as perfect as possible in meeting the needs of the imperfect person you married, because the only person you can change in a marriage is yourself!

Here's the caution: NEVER entertain the idea that you married the wrong person. Just don't go there! If you do, you'll start noticing the negatives and they will taint all the good things about your mate. Soon you'll find yourself on the hunt for someone "better" while your marriage goes spiraling downward.

Instead tell yourself, "I married Mr. (or Mrs.) Right for me." Then focus on being that person's "perfect" mate.

"We all stumble in many ways. If anyone is never at fault in what he says, he is a perfect man, able to keep his whole body in check." —James 3:2, NIV

DR. KAY KUZMA

A Rose of Love

Years ago I found a love poem by Douglas Malloch that spoke to me. I handwrote it on paper, illustrated, and framed it, and gave it to the love of my life on our wedding day.

A rose within a crystal glass, a rose to wither and to pass,
It's beauty fades, its glory goes—I know no way to keep a rose.
And yet there is a rose that blooms forever more in quiet rooms,
A rose within a fairer vase than purchased in the marketplace
The rose is love, the vase the home, a rose that blossoms when we roam
And when return, one rose God made that need not wither, need not fade.
And yet to keep that one rose fair the heart must also give it care,
Must nurture it with things like this; the morning smile, the goodnight kiss.
Aye, this is all this red rose needs, words of affection, helpful deeds,
Labors divided, burdens shared, and eyes that look as though they cared.
The rose of love will bow its head in rooms where angry words are said.
That rose will brave the wintry sky, but when hearts chill that rose will die.
If you the rose of love possess, keep it alive with tenderness,
And crystal pure with gentle hands the vase called home in which it stands.
There is one rose, the rose of love, you need not know the fading of,
A rose that watered day by day, you never need to throw away.

"I am the rose of Sharon, and the lily of the valleys. Like a lily among thorns,
so is my love among the daughters." —Song of Solomon 2:1, 2, NKJV

Why Most Women Resist Moving

Cutting ties to the past can be difficult—especially for a woman.

It's ironic that men, who are usually the primary breadwinners, have an easier time emotionally uprooting and moving to another location, even though it may be more difficult for them to find a comparable job! That's why men find it so hard to understand why their wives resist leaving the security of their surroundings.

Try to understand what the investment of a house means to a woman. Within it she finds security. Supportive friends are hard to replace. And it's tough to leave all the memories behind.

Job security is also important, especially as a woman gets older. Will she be able to find work she likes with the same benefits if they move to another location?

So men, if you're ready to move on to new frontiers and your wife's putting on the brakes, be understanding, won't you? Don't rip her security blanket away without first finding a good replacement!

"By faith Abraham obeyed when he was called. . . . And he went out, not knowing where he was going."
—Hebrews 11:8, NKJV

DR. KAY KUZMA

Role-Gender Scripts

When George and Becky got married, Becky made her husband number one. It was tough when she realized that she was often number two in George's life. When she complained, he explained, "I have to put work first. How could I expect you to love me if I can't support you?"

Laura grew up thinking that she could be superwoman and successfully carry the double responsibility of family and career. Ben had the expectation that a wife should be there to meet her husband's needs and shouldn't work outside the home. The sparks often flew!

Briana thought it was a woman's job to keep the house clean and was constantly picking up, mopping, vacuuming, and washing. Alex wanted a comfortable home where he could live, not a showplace or museum.

When you experience conflict because of different role expectations, don't blame your spouse. He or she is only following society and family scripts. Instead, reexamine your expectations and choose to compromise for the good of each other. In your marriage, there is only one right role expectation, and that's doing whatever is necessary to meet each other's needs.

"And my God will meet all your needs according to his glorious riches in Christ Jesus." —Philippians 4:19, NIV

A Time Not to Talk

The best way to solve a problem is to talk about it. Right? Well, not always. Sometimes it's best to act first and talk later.

After a rat streaked across Carrie's kitchen and disappeared into a cluttered closet, she screamed for her husband, Al. But because he was a perfectionist, she braced herself for his reaction to the messy closet.

Sure enough, he took one look inside and said, "What a mess! Why is there so much stuff in here?" After Carrie's angry reply, Al sat down to dialogue about the problem.

But Carrie was livid! Couldn't he see that he should kill the rat first?

It didn't take Al long to figure out his error and go after the rat. And they did sit down later and talk about the problem.

But the moral of this story is that when a rat is in the closet—or there is some other family crisis—it's no time to talk. It's time for action.

"A time to keep silence, and a time to speak" —Ecclesiastes 3:7, NKJV

DR. KAY KUZMA

Reach for the Stars

Some say that the reason so many marriages fail is that they have unrealistic ideals. Lower your standards, accept the fact that no marriage is perfect, and together work on solving daily disagreements so they don't mushroom into major conflicts.

That's probably wise counsel for mediocre marriages. But I like the philosophy that *ideals are like stars. You may never reach them, but you can set your course by them.* In other words, don't get discouraged because your marriage isn't perfect, but don't give up your goal for a more vibrant relationship just because it's not easy to obtain.

Share with each other the ideals you had when you were first married. Be truthful. Ask, "How is our marriage better than you dreamed possible? How is it different? What ideals are you beginning to think are impossible to reach, and why? What would we have to change in our marriage in order to reach our ideals?"

Pray about your ideals, ask God to soften your hearts to better meet each other's needs, and let your early ideals, like stars, guide you toward a more fulfilling marriage. God delights to make the impossible possible.

"I press toward the goal for the prize of the upward call of God in Christ Jesus." —Philippians 3:14, NKJV

The Riches of Family

One of my favorite proverbs is:

> "*Through wisdom a house is built,*
> *And by understanding it is established;*
> *By knowledge the rooms are filled*
> *With all precious and pleasant riches*"
> *(Proverbs 24:3, 4, NKJV).*

So many couples desire material possessions more than doing whatever it takes to better understand each other and their children. Here's a prayer you might want to consider:

"Lord, sometimes I think it would be nice to have all the latest gadgets, a boat or a new car, an iPad, trash compactor, or a hot tub. But I know what really counts: Quiet moments with my lover, fun activities that make our marriage more meaningful, and an abundant supply of hugs and kisses. So, please Lord, bless our family with Your abundant love. And give us the wisdom, understanding, and knowledge to fill the rooms of our home, not with material possessions, but with the precious and pleasant riches of meaningful relationships."

"*The fear of the* Lord *is the beginning of knowledge, but fools despise wisdom and instruction.*" —Proverbs 1:7, NKJV

DR. KAY KUZMA

INDEX

INDEX

INDEX

INDEX

INDEX

How to Listen With Love

Too often we think of talking as the way to be actively involved in a conversation. But if you listen right, listening can be active. In fact, it might just be that listening can be the best way to get the "I love you" message across to your mate.

Lean forward, look interested, and don't be afraid of periods of silence. It will give your spouse a chance to think, and hopefully, he or she will make the next response. Caution! If silence makes you feel uncomfortable and you think you need to fill up every moment of the conversation, you'll end up controlling it.

Then respond appropriately, sharing your own ideas when it will help to further your mutual understanding.

It takes time and work to listen actively. But it's the only kind of listening that will give the "I love you" message.

"He who answers a matter before he hears it, it is folly and shame to him." —Proverbs 18:13, NKJV

Who Is the Real Leader?

You've heard the joke that although the man is the head of the family, his wife is the neck that turns the head. Who IS the real leader of your family?

I have a feeling most men would identify with the cartoon I saw the other day that pictured a frustrated person frantically looking around, asking, "Which way did they go? How many of them were there? How fast were they going? I MUST find them; I am their LEADER!"

If you feel your family is leaving you behind, maybe it's time to re-evaluate your leadership skills. First of all, a leader gets involved. A leader has a vision for the family, communicating how to reach the goals, and helping when needed. A leader listens to the concerns of others and knows how to lift up and encourage.

Any woman married to a man with those kind of leadership skills isn't going to want to be the neck. She's going to be perfectly satisfied to stand beside him and be the helpmate God created her to be.

"For the husband is head of the wife, as also Christ is head of the church." —Ephesians 5:23, NKJV

DR. KAY KUZMA

Cleave and Leave

D on't let your marriage be destroyed by a meddling mother, an overbearing father, or an opinionated grandparent. There's wisdom in the biblical advice to cleave to your wife or husband and leave your family of origin. In today's world, that means, don't live with your parents—or even close to your parents—if they can't keep their mouths shut!

Husbands and wives shouldn't have to compete with the in-laws for their spouses' attention. Mothers and fathers shouldn't meddle. Parents don't have to know everything about their son's or daughter's lives once they are married. And they don't have to give their opinions, unless asked.

Too many grown kids remain tied to their parents' apron strings after they are married. Here's the fact. You can't grow closer to your mate, unless you let go of your mom and dad. You don't have to hurt them or totally ignore them; but just as good fences make good neighbors, good boundaries between a married couple and their families of origin, make good marriages.

"Therefore shall a man leave his father and his mother, and shall cleave unto his wife:
and they shall be one flesh." —Genesis 2:24, KJV

Couple Ministry for the Rejected

Are you looking for a ministry you can do with your spouse? Think about encouraging friends who are suffering from the rejection of separation or divorce.

There is no experience, other than death, that is so devastating to a person than divorce. Yet many find themselves not only divorced from their spouses, but divorced from their friends as well. One reason is because of the perception that the divorced single is on the lookout for a spouse, and therefore a potential threat to the marriages of others. Another reason that married couples state is that since both of the divorced were friends, to speak to one would offend the other.

Don't reject your divorced friends. As a couple, let your ministry be to encourage them. Let them know that you still accept them as individuals. Invite them to be a part of your family. Take time to listen. Don't try to counsel or act as a go-between. Be friends to both parties. Your friends need you.

"I want them to be encouraged and knit together by strong ties of love. I want them to have complete confidence that they understand God's mysterious plan, which is Christ himself." —Colossians 2:2, NLT

DR. KAY KUZMA